£3.25

SPIDER-MAN
Annual

Published by

MARVEL COMICS LIMITED
in association with
GRANDREAMS LIMITED
Jadwin House, 205/211 Kentish Town Road, London NW5 2JU.

Printed in Holland.

ISBN 0 86227 305 6

SPIDER-MAN
VERSUS
THE STRANGEST FOE OF ALL TIME...
DOCTOR OCTOPUS
DOCTOR OCTOPUS THE ONLY ENEMY EVER TO DEFEAT SPIDER-MAN!
IN THIS EPIC TALE... SEE THE HUMAN TORCH!
FANTASY! THRILLS!
STORY - STAN LEE
ART - STEVE DITKO
LETTERS - JOHN DUFFY
COLOR - ANDY YANCHUS
AND NOW BEGIN!

A STORY HAS TO START SOMEWHERE, SO LET'S BEGIN WITH A LONELY WAREHOUSE, IN THE DEAD OF NIGHT, WHERE WE FIND A ROBBERY TAKING PLACE...
HOLD IT, YOU GUYS! I THINK I HEARD SOMETHIN'!
RELAX, CHARLIE! IT WAS PROBABLY JUST A MOUSE!
SUDDENLY, THE MOST AWESOME IMAGE IN CRIME-FIGHTING APPEARS ON THE WALL DIRECTLY ABOVE THE STARTLED THIEVES...
MOUSE? YOU'VE NEVER SEEN A MOUSE LIKE THIS BEFORE!
LOOK!! IT--IT'S--
DON'T BE SHY, FELLA! YOU CAN SAY MY NAME! IT'S SPIDER-MAN!
GET 'IM! THERE ARE THREE OF US! HE CAN'T TAKE US ALL!
UGH!
BROTHER, YOU'RE LIVING IN A FOOL'S PARADISE!
OOF!
OW!
MINUTES LATER...
SOME BIG CRIMINAL MASTER-MIND YOU ARE!
AW, SHADDUP! WHOEVER EXPECTED SPIDER-MAN TO BUTT IN!
LOOK, JOE! SPIDER-MAN'S BEEN HERE! AND HOW!
AND, NOT FAR AWAY...
IT'S ALMOST TOO EASY! I'VE RUN OUT OF ENEMIES WHO CAN GIVE ME ANY REAL OPPOSITION! I'M TOO POWERFUL FOR ANY FOE! I ALMOST WISH FOR AN OPPONENT WHO'D GIVE ME A RUN FOR MY MONEY!
2

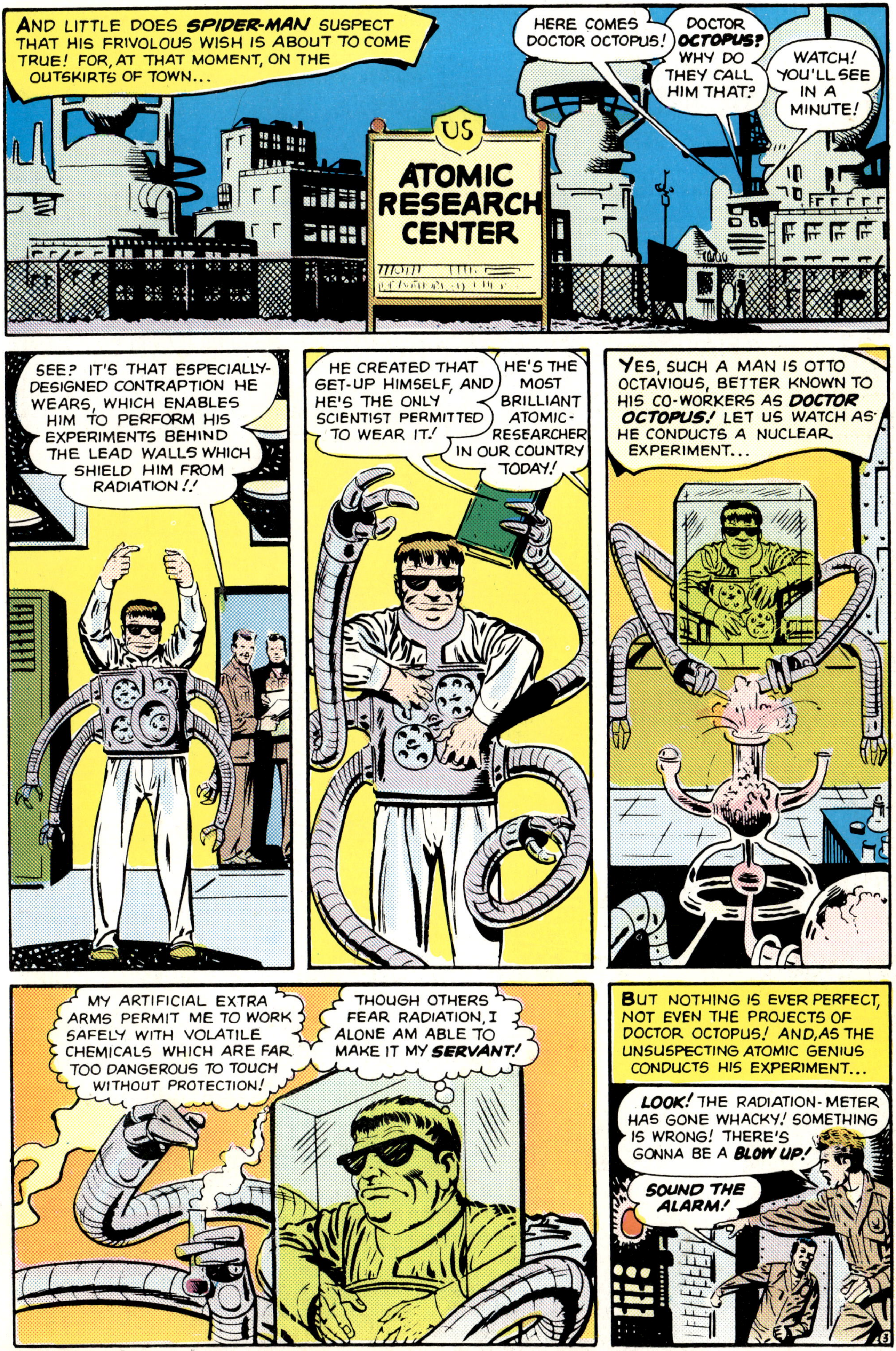
AND LITTLE DOES SPIDER-MAN SUSPECT THAT HIS FRIVOLOUS WISH IS ABOUT TO COME TRUE! FOR, AT THAT MOMENT, ON THE OUTSKIRTS OF TOWN...
HERE COMES DOCTOR OCTOPUS!
DOCTOR OCTOPUS? WHY DO THEY CALL HIM THAT?
WATCH! YOU'LL SEE IN A MINUTE!
US
ATOMIC RESEARCH CENTER
SEE? IT'S THAT ESPECIALLY-DESIGNED CONTRAPTION HE WEARS, WHICH ENABLES HIM TO PERFORM HIS EXPERIMENTS BEHIND THE LEAD WALLS WHICH SHIELD HIM FROM RADIATION!!
HE CREATED THAT GET-UP HIMSELF, AND HE'S THE ONLY SCIENTIST PERMITTED TO WEAR IT!
HE'S THE MOST BRILLIANT ATOMIC-RESEARCHER IN OUR COUNTRY TODAY!
YES, SUCH A MAN IS OTTO OCTAVIOUS, BETTER KNOWN TO HIS CO-WORKERS AS DOCTOR OCTOPUS! LET US WATCH AS HE CONDUCTS A NUCLEAR EXPERIMENT...
MY ARTIFICIAL EXTRA ARMS PERMIT ME TO WORK SAFELY WITH VOLATILE CHEMICALS WHICH ARE FAR TOO DANGEROUS TO TOUCH WITHOUT PROTECTION!
THOUGH OTHERS FEAR RADIATION, I ALONE AM ABLE TO MAKE IT MY SERVANT!
BUT NOTHING IS EVER PERFECT, NOT EVEN THE PROJECTS OF DOCTOR OCTOPUS! AND, AS THE UNSUSPECTING ATOMIC GENIUS CONDUCTS HIS EXPERIMENT...
LOOK! THE RADIATION-METER HAS GONE WHACKY! SOMETHING IS WRONG! THERE'S GONNA BE A BLOW UP!
SOUND THE ALARM!
3

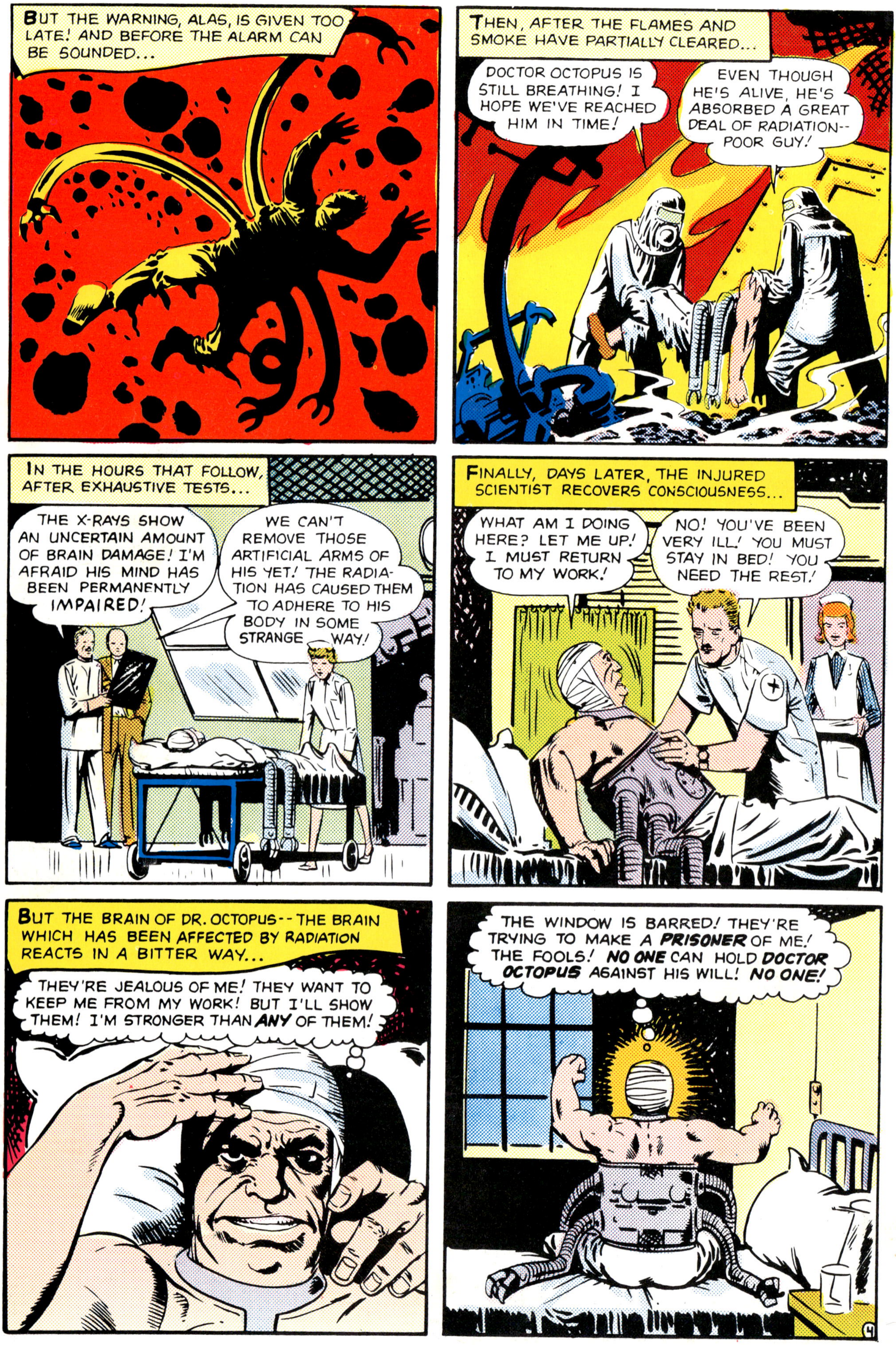
BUT THE WARNING, ALAS, IS GIVEN TOO LATE! AND BEFORE THE ALARM CAN BE SOUNDED...
THEN, AFTER THE FLAMES AND SMOKE HAVE PARTIALLY CLEARED...
DOCTOR OCTOPUS IS STILL BREATHING! I HOPE WE'VE REACHED HIM IN TIME!
EVEN THOUGH HE'S ALIVE, HE'S ABSORBED A GREAT DEAL OF RADIATION-- POOR GUY!
IN THE HOURS THAT FOLLOW, AFTER EXHAUSTIVE TESTS...
THE X-RAYS SHOW AN UNCERTAIN AMOUNT OF BRAIN DAMAGE! I'M AFRAID HIS MIND HAS BEEN PERMANENTLY IMPAIRED!
WE CAN'T REMOVE THOSE ARTIFICIAL ARMS OF HIS YET! THE RADIATION HAS CAUSED THEM TO ADHERE TO HIS BODY IN SOME STRANGE WAY!
FINALLY, DAYS LATER, THE INJURED SCIENTIST RECOVERS CONSCIOUSNESS...
WHAT AM I DOING HERE? LET ME UP! I MUST RETURN TO MY WORK!
NO! YOU'VE BEEN VERY ILL! YOU MUST STAY IN BED! YOU NEED THE REST!
BUT THE BRAIN OF DR. OCTOPUS-- THE BRAIN WHICH HAS BEEN AFFECTED BY RADIATION REACTS IN A BITTER WAY...
THEY'RE JEALOUS OF ME! THEY WANT TO KEEP ME FROM MY WORK! BUT I'LL SHOW THEM! I'M STRONGER THAN ANY OF THEM!
THE WINDOW IS BARRED! THEY'RE TRYING TO MAKE A PRISONER OF ME! THE FOOLS! NO ONE CAN HOLD DOCTOR OCTOPUS AGAINST HIS WILL! NO ONE!
4

THEN SUDDENLY, AT JUST A SUGGESTION OF A THOUGHT BY DR. OCTOPUS, HIS ARTIFICIAL ARMS MOVE AS THOUGH THEY HAVE A WILL OF THEIR OWN...
I'VE GOT TO BREAK THOSE BARS!
I DID IT!! MY ARMS DID IT! THEIR STRENGTH IS INCALCULABLE! THEY CAN DO ANYTHING!!
SOMEHOW, MY MECHANICAL ARMS HAVE ALMOST BECOME A PART OF ME! THEY OBEY MY EVERY COMMAND! WITH SUCH POWER AND MY BRILLIANT MIND, I'M THE SUPREME HUMAN BEING ON EARTH!
MINUTES LATER...
YOU WANTED TO SEE ME, DR. OCTOPUS?
YES! COME IN! SHUT THE DOOR BEHIND YOU!
WHAT IS IT? YOU-- OH, NO! NO!
HA-HA! YOU DON'T BELIEVE WHAT YOU SEE? BUT IT'S TRUE! I'M ALL-POWERFUL! FROM NOW ON, I GIVE THE COMMANDS HERE!
MEANWHILE, AT THE OFFICE OF J. JONAH JAMESON, PUBLISHER OF THE DAILY BUGLE...
I WANT PICTURES OF THE INJURED SCIENTIST, DR. OCTOPUS, BUT NO ONE IS ALLOWED TO ENTER THE BLISS PRIVATE HOSPITAL ANY MORE!
I NEVER HEARD OF ANY HOSPITAL KEEPING PEOPLE OUT! DON'T WORRY, J.J.! I'LL GET THOSE PIX FOR YOU!
MY BEST MEN HAVE TRIED AND FAILED! BUT SO FAR, YOU'VE SUCCEEDED IN EVERY ASSIGNMENT! I CAN'T IMAGINE HOW A TEEN-AGER LIKE YOU DOES IT!
OUR AGREEMENT, J.J., IS THAT YOU'RE NEVER TO ASK ME HOW I DO IT!
JUST HAVE A CHECK READY FOR ME WHEN I BRING BACK THE PIX OF DR. OCTOPUS!
HE DOESN'T SUSPECT PETER PARKER, THE TEENAGER HE ASSIGNED TO THE JOB, IS GONNA HAVE SPIDER-MAN DO IT!
5

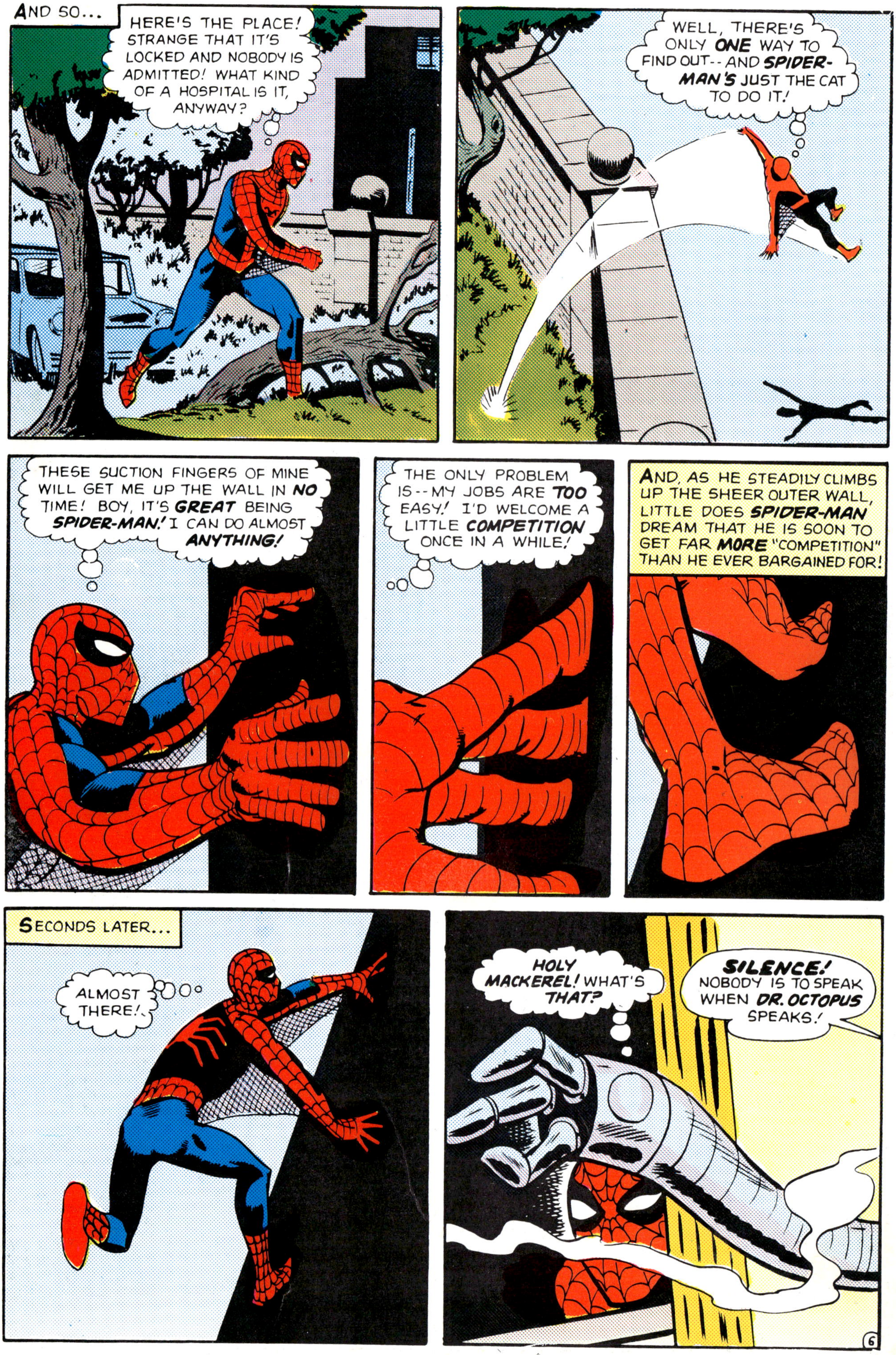
AND SO...
HERE'S THE PLACE! STRANGE THAT IT'S LOCKED AND NOBODY IS ADMITTED! WHAT KIND OF A HOSPITAL IS IT, ANYWAY?
WELL, THERE'S ONLY ONE WAY TO FIND OUT-- AND SPIDER-MAN'S JUST THE CAT TO DO IT!
THESE SUCTION FINGERS OF MINE WILL GET ME UP THE WALL IN NO TIME! BOY, IT'S GREAT BEING SPIDER-MAN! I CAN DO ALMOST ANYTHING!
THE ONLY PROBLEM IS-- MY JOBS ARE TOO EASY! I'D WELCOME A LITTLE COMPETITION ONCE IN A WHILE!
AND, AS HE STEADILY CLIMBS UP THE SHEER OUTER WALL, LITTLE DOES SPIDER-MAN DREAM THAT HE IS SOON TO GET FAR MORE "COMPETITION" THAN HE EVER BARGAINED FOR!
SECONDS LATER...
ALMOST THERE!
HOLY MACKEREL! WHAT'S THAT?
SILENCE! NOBODY IS TO SPEAK WHEN DR. OCTOPUS SPEAKS!
6

PEERING UNSEEN THROUGH THE LARGE PICTURE-WINDOW, SPIDER-MAN WITNESSES A STRANGE, UNEXPECTED SIGHT...
YOU CAN'T KEEP ALL OF US PRISONERS FOREVER, DOCTOR OCTOPUS! WE'VE DONE WHAT YOU ASKED-- GOTTEN YOU ALL THE EQUIPMENT YOU WANTED! WHEN WILL YOU LET US GO?
NOT UNTIL I'M READY! WITH MY POWERS, NO ONE CAN RESIST ME! YOU'LL REMAIN TO SERVE ME UNTIL I NO LONGER NEED YOU-- AND NOT BEFORE!
WELL, WELL! SO THE GOOD DOC HAS FLIPPED HIS LID, EH? WELL, THIS IS JUST WHAT I'VE BEEN HOPIN' FOR-- A LITTLE ACTION!
BUT THIS IS MAD! YOU HAVE NO RIGHT--
RIGHT?! YOU DARE SPEAK TO ME OF RIGHT?
I HAVE THE RIGHT TO DO ANYTHING-- AS LONG AS I HAVE THE POWER! AND IF YOU DOUBT MY POWER, HERE IS A SMALL SAMPLE...
NO! DON'T! LET ME DOWN!
LOOKS LIKE IT'S TIME FOR SPIDER-MAN TO JOIN THE PARTY BEFORE HE REALLY HURTS THAT FELLA!
HOLD IT, DOC! HOW ABOUT PICKIN' ON SOMEONE WHO CAN FIGHT YOU BACK?
SPIDER-MAN!
WELL, I SURE AIN'T ALBERT SCHWEITZER!
YOU DARE SPEAK FLIPPANTLY TO ME? YOU FOOL! WHEN I'M FINISHED WITH YOU, YOU'LL SING A DIFFERENT TUNE!
7

YOU DON'T THINK THOSE DUMB-LOOKING FLAPPERS OF YOURS CAN MOVE FAST ENOUGH TO CATCH SPIDER-MAN, DO YOU?
HEY!! WHA--?
SURPRISED? DOCTOR OCTOPUS IS FAR MORE POWERFUL THAN YOU DREAMED! FAR MORE POWERFUL THAN EVEN YOU!
DON'T LET THAT ONE LUCKY PUNCH GO TO YOUR HEAD, PAL! I'VE A FEW MORE SURPRISES!
AH! MOST INGENIOUS OF YOU! YOUR SPIDER'S WEB!!
BUT, AS YOU CAN SEE, HOLDING ONLY TWO OF MY ARMS ISN'T ENOUGH! I STILL HAVE MORE!
NO TIME TO SHOOT MY WEB AGAIN! HE'S FASTER THAN I EXPECTED!
BUT I CAN STILL GRAB HIS OTHER ARMS!
OOF! IT TAKES ALL MY STRENGTH! HE--HE ALSO HAS SUPER-HUMAN POWER!
MY WEB! HE SNAPPED IT! NOBODY HAS EVER DONE THAT BEFORE!
AND NOW, SPIDER-MAN, I GROW BORED WITH THIS GAME! MY TIME IS TOO VALUABLE!
8

NOW, WATCH ME TRAP A SPIDER IN A WEB OF MY OWN-- A WEB MADE OF MY NEW-FOUND ARMS! YOUR STRENGTH IS MERELY THAT OF A SPIDER, BUT MINE IS THE ENERGY OF AN ATOM, BORN OF A NUCLEAR ACCIDENT!
I'M HELPLESS! CAN'T FIGHT ALL THOSE ARMS AT ONCE! DON'T KNOW WHAT TO DO NEXT! HE'S JUST TOYING WITH ME!
YOU DARED TO MOCK ME BEFORE! WHY AREN'T YOU MOCKING ME NOW? WHERE ARE YOUR BRAVE WORDS AND TAUNTS NOW, SPIDER-MAN?
OR DO YOU REALIZE YOU'VE FINALLY MET YOUR MASTER? AND NOW, YOU CAN LEAVE THE WAY YOU ENTERED! YOU'RE NO THREAT TO ME!
WEAK, GROGGY, JUST BARELY CONSCIOUS, SPIDER-MAN HAS HIS FALL BROKEN BY A TREE, AS HE FINALLY SLUMPS TO THE GROUND... IN DEFEAT!
9

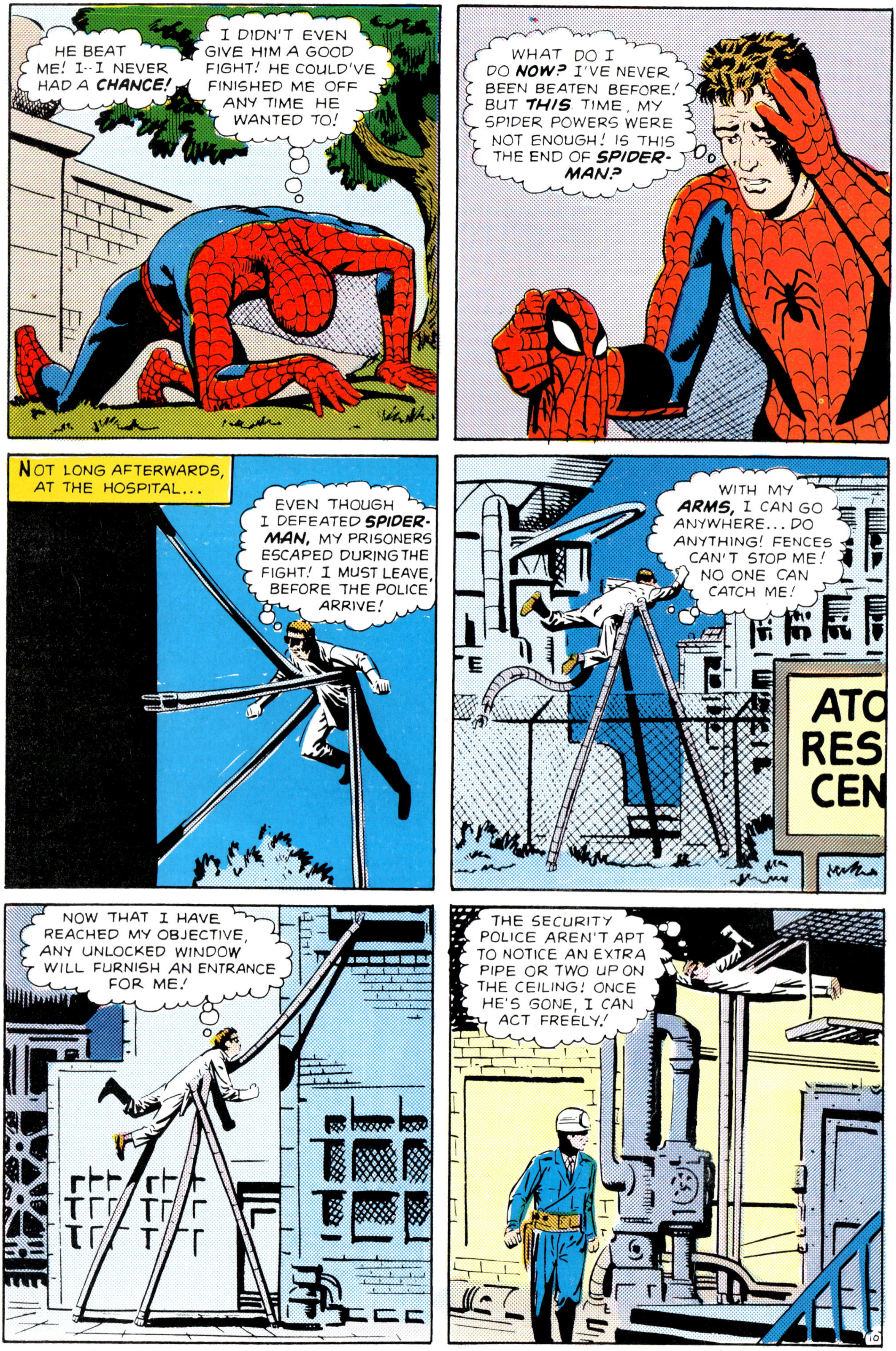
HE BEAT ME! I--I NEVER HAD A CHANCE!
I DIDN'T EVEN GIVE HIM A GOOD FIGHT! HE COULD'VE FINISHED ME OFF ANY TIME HE WANTED TO!
WHAT DO I DO NOW? I'VE NEVER BEEN BEATEN BEFORE! BUT THIS TIME, MY SPIDER POWERS WERE NOT ENOUGH! IS THIS THE END OF SPIDER-MAN?
NOT LONG AFTERWARDS, AT THE HOSPITAL...
EVEN THOUGH I DEFEATED SPIDER-MAN, MY PRISONERS ESCAPED DURING THE FIGHT! I MUST LEAVE, BEFORE THE POLICE ARRIVE!
WITH MY ARMS, I CAN GO ANYWHERE... DO ANYTHING! FENCES CAN'T STOP ME! NO ONE CAN CATCH ME!
ATO
RES
CEN
NOW THAT I HAVE REACHED MY OBJECTIVE, ANY UNLOCKED WINDOW WILL FURNISH AN ENTRANCE FOR ME!
THE SECURITY POLICE AREN'T APT TO NOTICE AN EXTRA PIPE OR TWO UP ON THE CEILING! ONCE HE'S GONE, I CAN ACT FREELY!
10

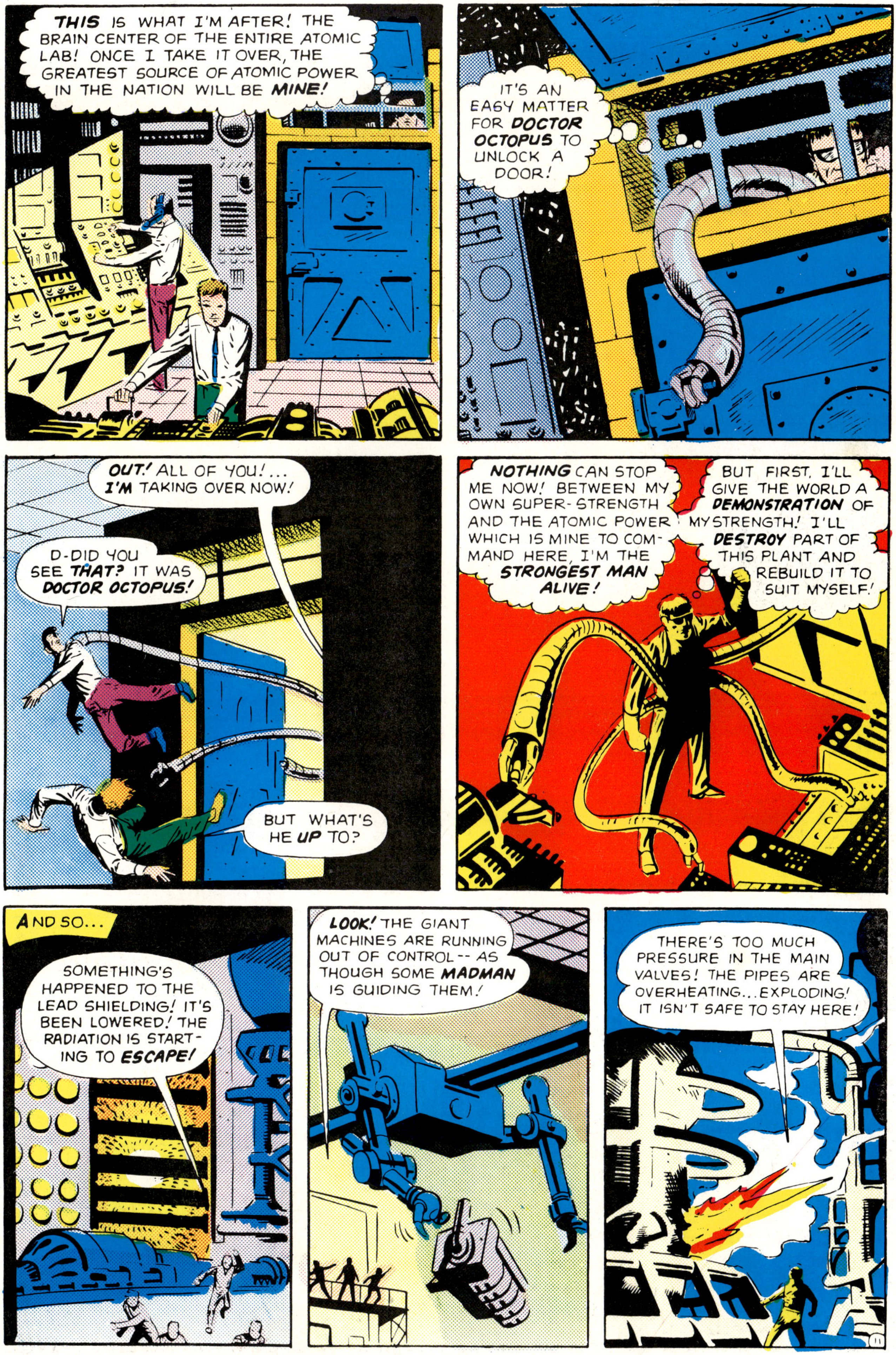
THIS IS WHAT I'M AFTER! THE BRAIN CENTER OF THE ENTIRE ATOMIC LAB! ONCE I TAKE IT OVER, THE GREATEST SOURCE OF ATOMIC POWER IN THE NATION WILL BE MINE!
IT'S AN EASY MATTER FOR DOCTOR OCTOPUS TO UNLOCK A DOOR!
OUT! ALL OF YOU!... I'M TAKING OVER NOW!
D-DID YOU SEE THAT? IT WAS DOCTOR OCTOPUS!
BUT WHAT'S HE UP TO?
NOTHING CAN STOP ME NOW! BETWEEN MY OWN SUPER-STRENGTH AND THE ATOMIC POWER WHICH IS MINE TO COMMAND HERE, I'M THE STRONGEST MAN ALIVE!
BUT FIRST, I'LL GIVE THE WORLD A DEMONSTRATION OF MY STRENGTH! I'LL DESTROY PART OF THIS PLANT AND REBUILD IT TO SUIT MYSELF!
AND SO...
SOMETHING'S HAPPENED TO THE LEAD SHIELDING! IT'S BEEN LOWERED! THE RADIATION IS STARTING TO ESCAPE!
LOOK! THE GIANT MACHINES ARE RUNNING OUT OF CONTROL -- AS THOUGH SOME MADMAN IS GUIDING THEM!
THERE'S TOO MUCH PRESSURE IN THE MAIN VALVES! THE PIPES ARE OVERHEATING... EXPLODING! IT ISN'T SAFE TO STAY HERE!
11

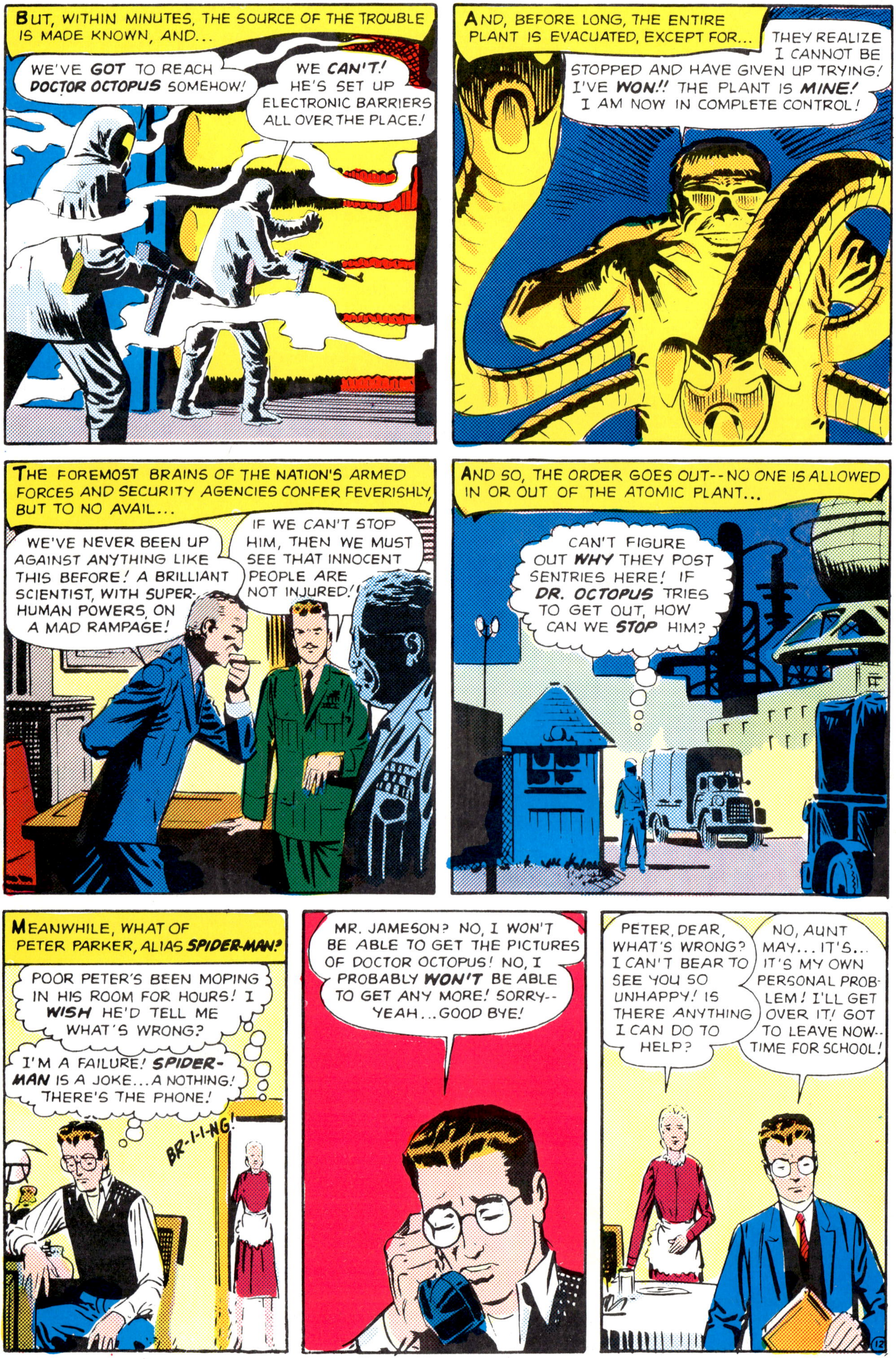

BUT, WITHIN MINUTES, THE SOURCE OF THE TROUBLE IS MADE KNOWN, AND...
WE'VE GOT TO REACH DOCTOR OCTOPUS SOMEHOW!
WE CAN'T! HE'S SET UP ELECTRONIC BARRIERS ALL OVER THE PLACE!
AND, BEFORE LONG, THE ENTIRE PLANT IS EVACUATED, EXCEPT FOR...
THEY REALIZE I CANNOT BE STOPPED AND HAVE GIVEN UP TRYING! I'VE WON!! THE PLANT IS MINE! I AM NOW IN COMPLETE CONTROL!
THE FOREMOST BRAINS OF THE NATION'S ARMED FORCES AND SECURITY AGENCIES CONFER FEVERISHLY, BUT TO NO AVAIL...
WE'VE NEVER BEEN UP AGAINST ANYTHING LIKE THIS BEFORE! A BRILLIANT SCIENTIST, WITH SUPER-HUMAN POWERS, ON A MAD RAMPAGE!
IF WE CAN'T STOP HIM, THEN WE MUST SEE THAT INNOCENT PEOPLE ARE NOT INJURED!
AND SO, THE ORDER GOES OUT--NO ONE IS ALLOWED IN OR OUT OF THE ATOMIC PLANT...
CAN'T FIGURE OUT WHY THEY POST SENTRIES HERE! IF DR. OCTOPUS TRIES TO GET OUT, HOW CAN WE STOP HIM?
MEANWHILE, WHAT OF PETER PARKER, ALIAS SPIDER-MAN?
POOR PETER'S BEEN MOPING IN HIS ROOM FOR HOURS! I WISH HE'D TELL ME WHAT'S WRONG?
I'M A FAILURE! SPIDER-MAN IS A JOKE... A NOTHING! THERE'S THE PHONE!
BR-I-I-NG!
MR. JAMESON? NO, I WON'T BE ABLE TO GET THE PICTURES OF DOCTOR OCTOPUS! NO, I PROBABLY WON'T BE ABLE TO GET ANY MORE! SORRY-- YEAH... GOOD BYE!
PETER, DEAR, WHAT'S WRONG? I CAN'T BEAR TO SEE YOU SO UNHAPPY! IS THERE ANYTHING I CAN DO TO HELP?
NO, AUNT MAY... IT'S... IT'S MY OWN PERSONAL PROBLEM! I'LL GET OVER IT! GOT TO LEAVE NOW-- TIME FOR SCHOOL!
12

HELLO, PETEY!... SAY, WHAT'S WITH HIM? HE DIDN'T ANSWER!
AND THERE'S NO ONE I CAN TALK TO... NO ONE WHO'D UNDERSTAND!
HIM? HE'S DOWN IN THE DUMPS! LOOKS LIKE HE LOST HIS FAVORITE TEST TUBE!
PETE, DID YOU HEAR THE BIG NEWS? THE GOVERNOR'S ASKED THE FANTASTIC FOUR TO TRY TO CAPTURE DOCTOR OCTOPUS!
THEY'RE BUSY WITH ANOTHER CASE, BUT THEY SENT THE HUMAN TORCH TO SEE WHAT HE CAN DO! HE'S SPEAKING TO OUR ASSEMBLY TODAY!
BIG DEAL!
LATER, AT THE SCHOOL ASSEMBLY...
I WAS ASKED HERE TO TACKLE DOCTOR OCTOPUS! BUT I'VE USED MY FLAME SO MUCH RECENTLY, I HAVE TO WAIT A FEW DAYS TO LET IT GET STRONG AGAIN! WHILE I'M WAITING, YOUR PRINCIPAL ASKED ME TO ADDRESS YOU...
IF ONLY I HAD HIS POWER... HIS CONFIDENCE!... BUT THAT'S EASY WHEN YOU'VE NEVER BEEN BEATEN!
NOW FOR A LITTLE DEMONSTRATION! I CAN'T APPLY MY TOTAL FLAME, BUT HERE ARE SOME FIERY FIGURES FOR YOU!
THIS IS WHAT USUALLY HAPPENS WHEN THE THING HELPS ME WITH MY HOMEWORK! I GET RESULTS LIKE THIS!
2
2
3
THEN, AFTER A FEW MORE COLORFUL DEMONSTRATIONS...
NOW, FOR A PARTING THOUGHT! STICK TO YOUR SCHOOL WORK AND DO YOUR BEST IN YOUR STUDIES! DON'T BE DISCOURAGED IF IT SOMETIMES SEEMS TOUGH! THE IMPORTANT THING IS NEVER GIVE UP! REMEMBER THAT--NEVER GIVE UP!
ABILITY ALONE ISN'T ENOUGH! IT'S ONE LESSON I'VE LEARNED FROM MY PARTNERSHIP WITH THE FANTASTIC FOUR!
IT'S ALMOST AS THOUGH HE'S TALKING TO ME!
EVEN THE FANTASTIC FOUR HAVE HAD DEFEATS--BUT WE ALWAYS COME BACK! OUR MOTTO IS NEVER SAY DIE!
HE'S RIGHT! BY GOLLY, HE'S RIGHT!
LATER, AT THE CONCLUSION OF THE TORCH'S LECTURE...
I WANT TO THANK YOU FOR THAT SPEECH! I--I'LL NEVER FORGET WHAT YOU SAID TODAY! IT MEANT A LOT TO ME!
HUH? OH, SURE--SURE! GLAD YOU ENJOYED IT, FELLA!
13

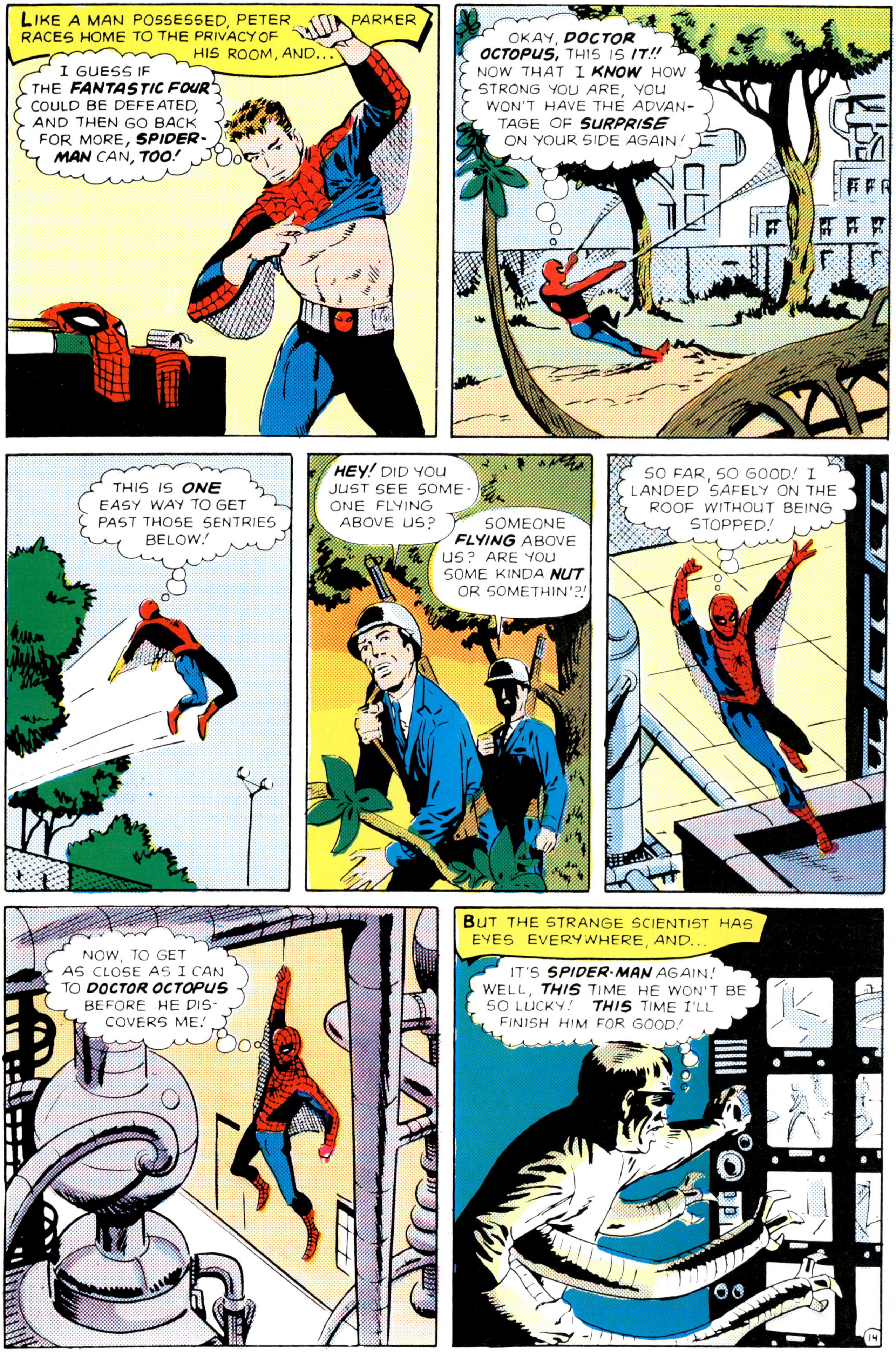
LIKE A MAN POSSESSED, PETER PARKER RACES HOME TO THE PRIVACY OF HIS ROOM, AND...
I GUESS IF THE FANTASTIC FOUR COULD BE DEFEATED, AND THEN GO BACK FOR MORE, SPIDER-MAN CAN, TOO!
OKAY, DOCTOR OCTOPUS, THIS IS IT!! NOW THAT I KNOW HOW STRONG YOU ARE, YOU WON'T HAVE THE ADVANTAGE OF SURPRISE ON YOUR SIDE AGAIN!
THIS IS ONE EASY WAY TO GET PAST THOSE SENTRIES BELOW!
HEY! DID YOU JUST SEE SOMEONE FLYING ABOVE US?
SOMEONE FLYING ABOVE US? ARE YOU SOME KINDA NUT OR SOMETHIN'?!
SO FAR, SO GOOD! I LANDED SAFELY ON THE ROOF WITHOUT BEING STOPPED!
NOW, TO GET AS CLOSE AS I CAN TO DOCTOR OCTOPUS BEFORE HE DISCOVERS ME!
BUT THE STRANGE SCIENTIST HAS EYES EVERYWHERE, AND...
IT'S SPIDER-MAN AGAIN! WELL, THIS TIME HE WON'T BE SO LUCKY! THIS TIME I'LL FINISH HIM FOR GOOD!
14

FROM NOW ON, I ALLOW NO ONE TO INTERFERE WITH MY PLANS! I WILL PERMIT NO ONE TO DEFY ME!
AND, AT THAT MOMENT...
MY SPIDER SENSES WARN ME OF DANGER BEHIND ME!
NICE TRY, DOCTOR OCTOPUS! BUT I'M READY FOR YOU THIS TIME!
WITH MY SPIDER SENSES FULLY ALERT, AND MY SPIDER MUSCLES IN TOP CONDITION, HE CAN'T POSSIBLY HURL THOSE ELECTRONIC BOLTS FAST ENOUGH TO HURT ME!
HE KNOWS MY EVERY MOVE! HE MUST BE WATCHING ME ON SOME SORT OF TV HOOK-UP! WELL, I'LL JUST GO SOMEWHERE OUT OF RANGE... AS ONLY I CAN!
HE'S FOUND A WAY TO EVADE MY ELECTRONIC SCANNERS! HMM... HE'S CLEVERER THAN I THOUGHT!
15

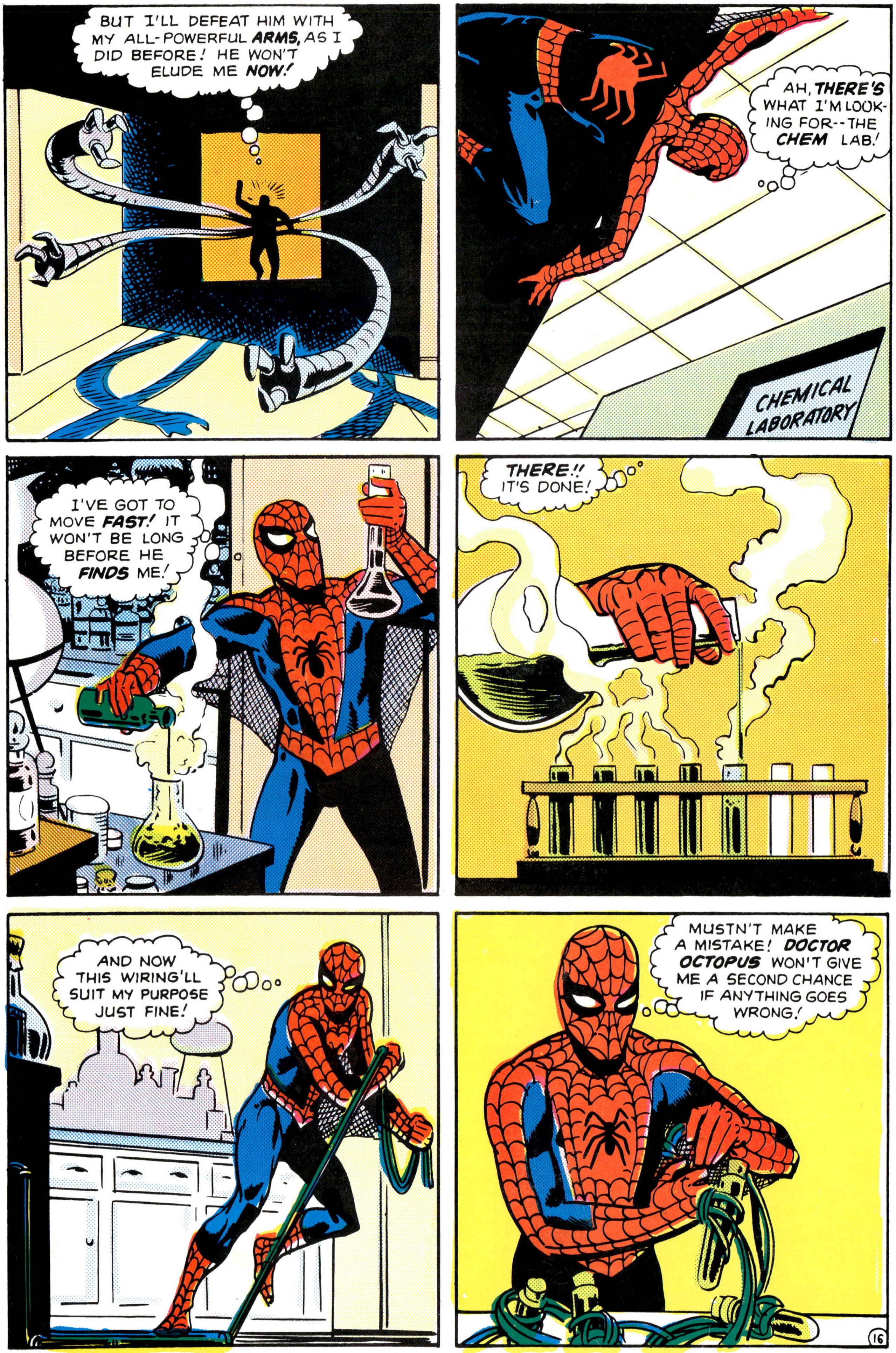
BUT I'LL DEFEAT HIM WITH MY ALL-POWERFUL ARMS, AS I DID BEFORE! HE WON'T ELUDE ME NOW!
AH, THERE'S WHAT I'M LOOKING FOR--THE CHEM LAB!
CHEMICAL LABORATORY
I'VE GOT TO MOVE FAST! IT WON'T BE LONG BEFORE HE FINDS ME!
THERE!! IT'S DONE!
AND NOW THIS WIRING'LL SUIT MY PURPOSE JUST FINE!
MUSTN'T MAKE A MISTAKE! DOCTOR OCTOPUS WON'T GIVE ME A SECOND CHANCE IF ANYTHING GOES WRONG!
16

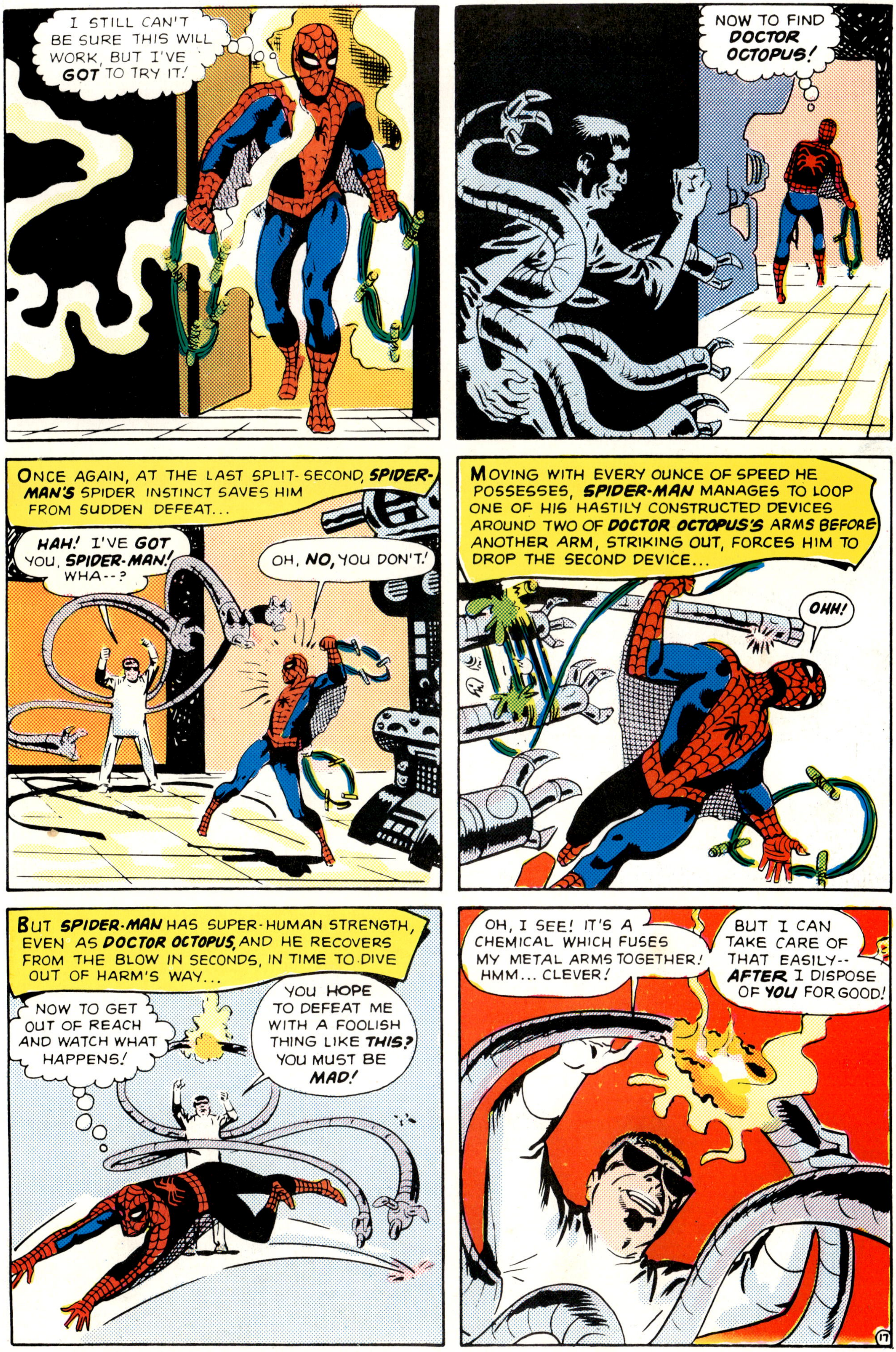
I STILL CAN'T BE SURE THIS WILL WORK, BUT I'VE **GOT** TO TRY IT!
NOW TO FIND **DOCTOR OCTOPUS!**
ONCE AGAIN, AT THE LAST SPLIT-SECOND, **SPIDER-MAN'S** SPIDER INSTINCT SAVES HIM FROM SUDDEN DEFEAT...
HAH! I'VE **GOT** YOU, **SPIDER-MAN!** WHA--?
OH, **NO,** YOU DON'T!
MOVING WITH EVERY OUNCE OF SPEED HE POSSESSES, **SPIDER-MAN** MANAGES TO LOOP ONE OF HIS HASTILY CONSTRUCTED DEVICES AROUND TWO OF **DOCTOR OCTOPUS'S** ARMS BEFORE ANOTHER ARM, STRIKING OUT, FORCES HIM TO DROP THE SECOND DEVICE...
OHH!
BUT **SPIDER-MAN** HAS SUPER-HUMAN STRENGTH, EVEN AS **DOCTOR OCTOPUS,** AND HE RECOVERS FROM THE BLOW IN SECONDS, IN TIME TO DIVE OUT OF HARM'S WAY...
NOW TO GET OUT OF REACH AND WATCH WHAT HAPPENS!
YOU **HOPE** TO DEFEAT ME WITH A FOOLISH THING LIKE **THIS?** YOU MUST BE **MAD!**
OH, I SEE! IT'S A CHEMICAL WHICH FUSES MY METAL ARMS TOGETHER! HMM... CLEVER!
BUT I CAN TAKE CARE OF THAT EASILY-- **AFTER** I DISPOSE OF **YOU** FOR GOOD!
17

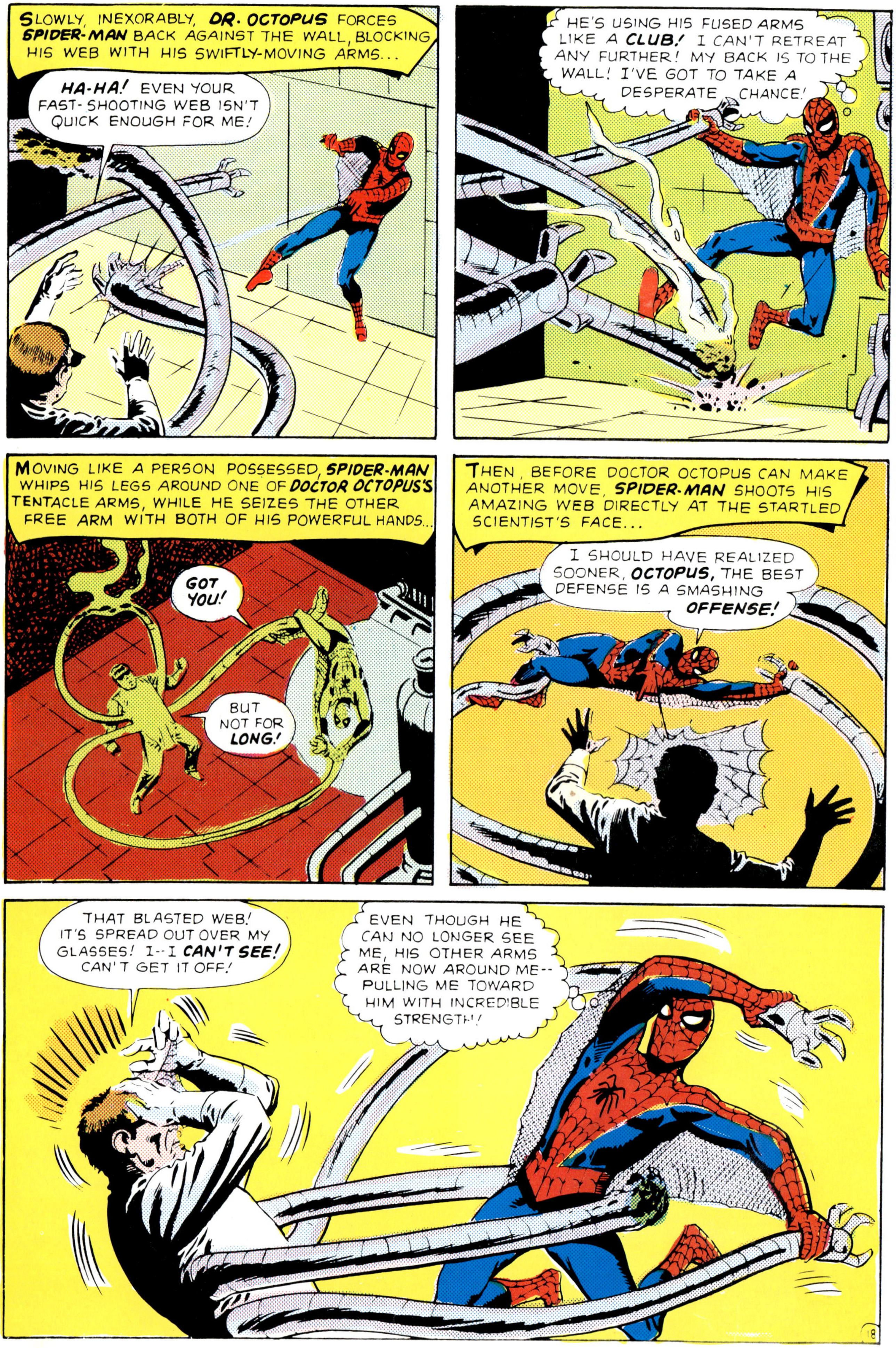
SLOWLY, INEXORABLY, DR. OCTOPUS FORCES SPIDER-MAN BACK AGAINST THE WALL, BLOCKING HIS WEB WITH HIS SWIFTLY-MOVING ARMS...
HA-HA! EVEN YOUR FAST-SHOOTING WEB ISN'T QUICK ENOUGH FOR ME!
HE'S USING HIS FUSED ARMS LIKE A CLUB! I CAN'T RETREAT ANY FURTHER! MY BACK IS TO THE WALL! I'VE GOT TO TAKE A DESPERATE CHANCE!
MOVING LIKE A PERSON POSSESSED, SPIDER-MAN WHIPS HIS LEGS AROUND ONE OF DOCTOR OCTOPUS'S TENTACLE ARMS, WHILE HE SEIZES THE OTHER FREE ARM WITH BOTH OF HIS POWERFUL HANDS...
GOT YOU!
BUT NOT FOR LONG!
THEN, BEFORE DOCTOR OCTOPUS CAN MAKE ANOTHER MOVE, SPIDER-MAN SHOOTS HIS AMAZING WEB DIRECTLY AT THE STARTLED SCIENTIST'S FACE...
I SHOULD HAVE REALIZED SOONER, OCTOPUS, THE BEST DEFENSE IS A SMASHING OFFENSE!
THAT BLASTED WEB! IT'S SPREAD OUT OVER MY GLASSES! I--I CAN'T SEE! CAN'T GET IT OFF!
EVEN THOUGH HE CAN NO LONGER SEE ME, HIS OTHER ARMS ARE NOW AROUND ME-- PULLING ME TOWARD HIM WITH INCREDIBLE STRENGTH!
18

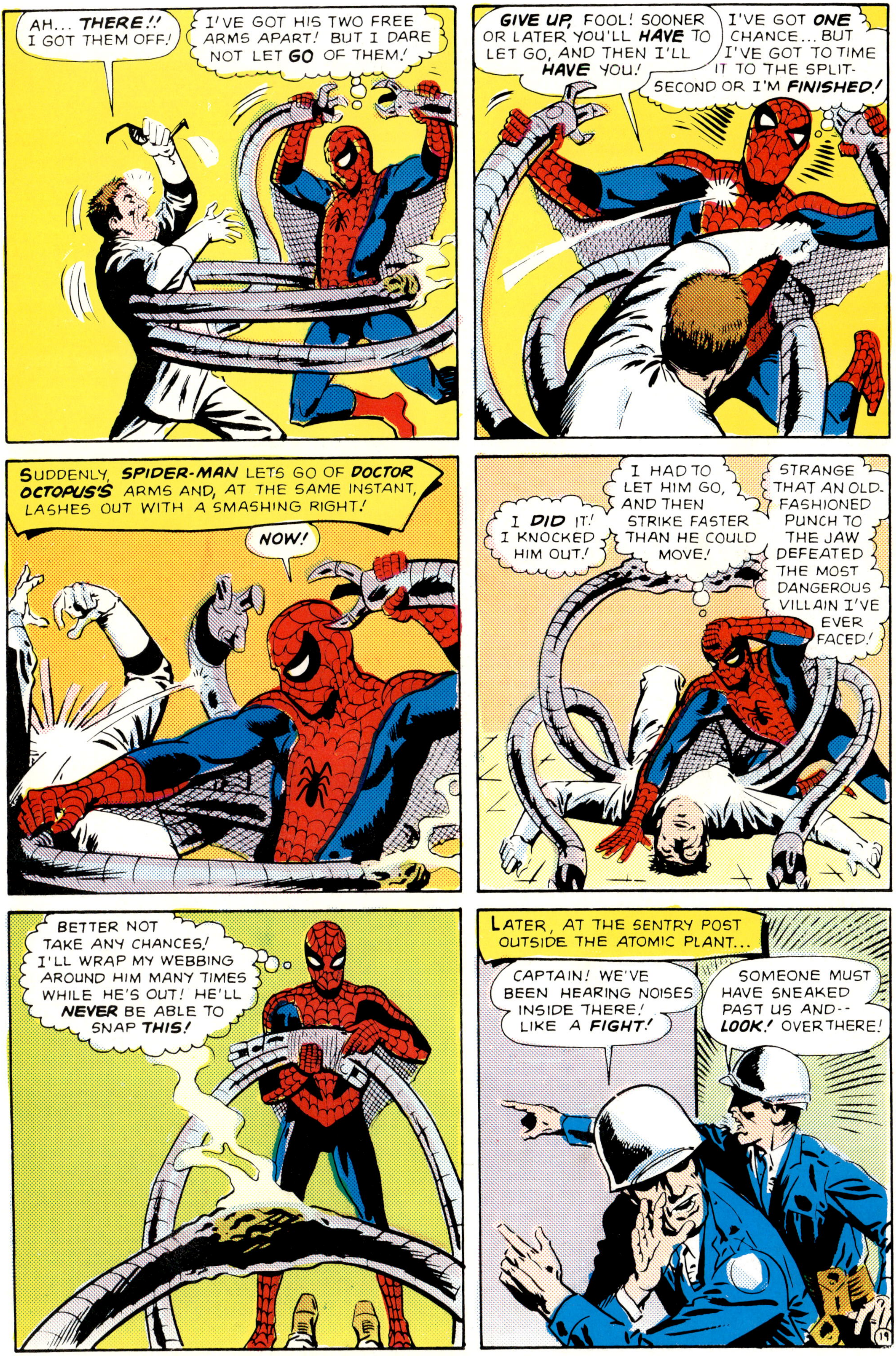

AH... THERE!! I GOT THEM OFF!
I'VE GOT HIS TWO FREE ARMS APART! BUT I DARE NOT LET GO OF THEM!
GIVE UP, FOOL! SOONER OR LATER YOU'LL HAVE TO LET GO, AND THEN I'LL HAVE YOU!
I'VE GOT ONE CHANCE... BUT I'VE GOT TO TIME IT TO THE SPLIT-SECOND OR I'M FINISHED!
SUDDENLY, SPIDER-MAN LETS GO OF DOCTOR OCTOPUS'S ARMS AND, AT THE SAME INSTANT, LASHES OUT WITH A SMASHING RIGHT!
NOW!
I DID IT! I KNOCKED HIM OUT!
I HAD TO LET HIM GO, AND THEN STRIKE FASTER THAN HE COULD MOVE!
STRANGE THAT AN OLD-FASHIONED PUNCH TO THE JAW DEFEATED THE MOST DANGEROUS VILLAIN I'VE EVER FACED!
BETTER NOT TAKE ANY CHANCES! I'LL WRAP MY WEBBING AROUND HIM MANY TIMES WHILE HE'S OUT! HE'LL NEVER BE ABLE TO SNAP THIS!
LATER, AT THE SENTRY POST OUTSIDE THE ATOMIC PLANT...
CAPTAIN! WE'VE BEEN HEARING NOISES INSIDE THERE! LIKE A FIGHT!
SOMEONE MUST HAVE SNEAKED PAST US AND-- LOOK! OVER THERE!
19

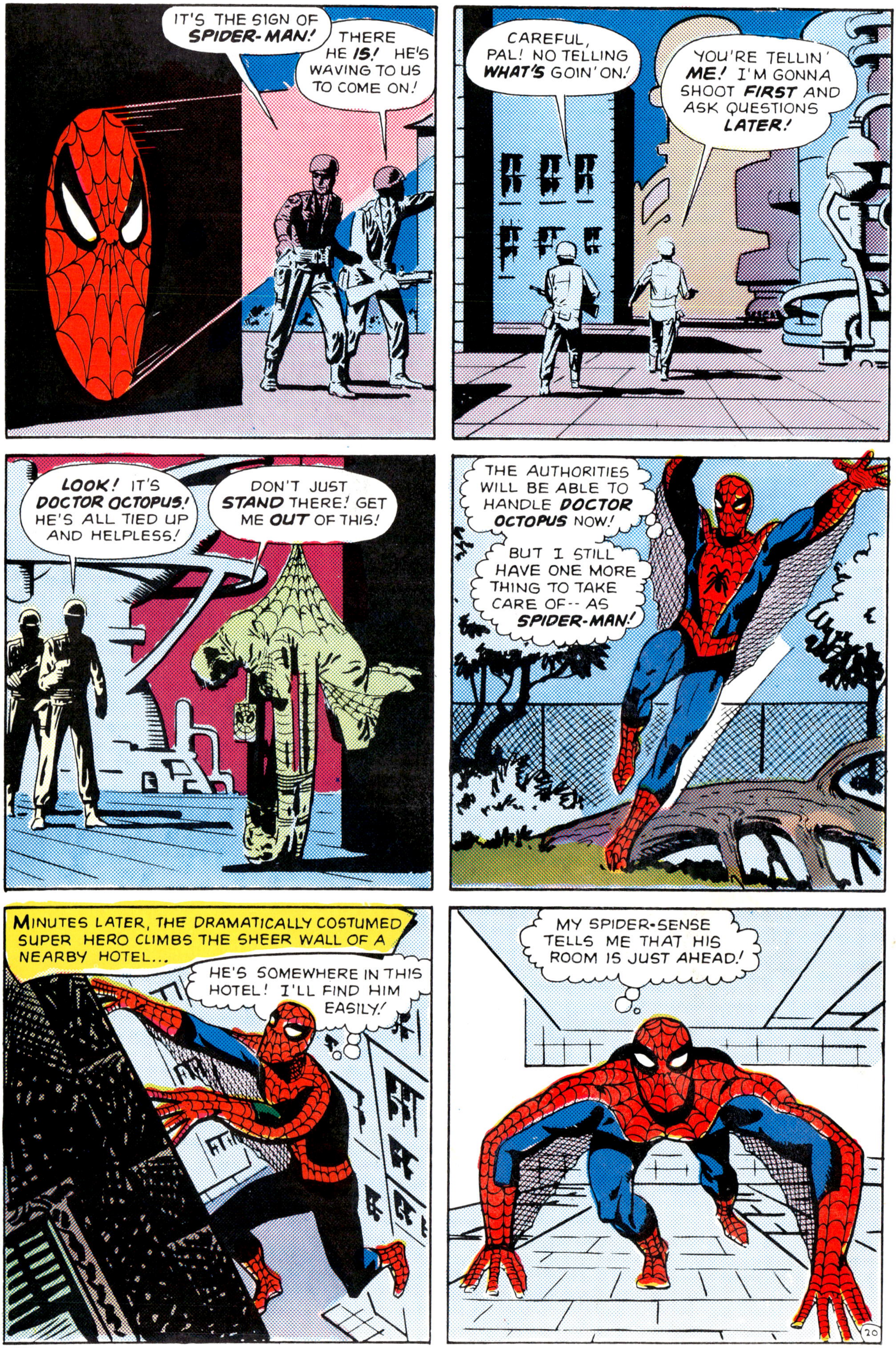

IT'S THE SIGN OF SPIDER-MAN!
THERE HE IS! HE'S WAVING TO US TO COME ON!
CAREFUL, PAL! NO TELLING WHAT'S GOIN' ON!
YOU'RE TELLIN' ME! I'M GONNA SHOOT FIRST AND ASK QUESTIONS LATER!
LOOK! IT'S DOCTOR OCTOPUS! HE'S ALL TIED UP AND HELPLESS!
DON'T JUST STAND THERE! GET ME OUT OF THIS!
THE AUTHORITIES WILL BE ABLE TO HANDLE DOCTOR OCTOPUS NOW!
BUT I STILL HAVE ONE MORE THING TO TAKE CARE OF-- AS SPIDER-MAN!
MINUTES LATER, THE DRAMATICALLY COSTUMED SUPER HERO CLIMBS THE SHEER WALL OF A NEARBY HOTEL...
HE'S SOMEWHERE IN THIS HOTEL! I'LL FIND HIM EASILY!
MY SPIDER-SENSE TELLS ME THAT HIS ROOM IS JUST AHEAD!
20

AND INSIDE THE ROOM IN QUESTION...
GOOD NEWS, TORCH! YOUR TEMPERATURE IS DOWN AND YOUR VIRUS IS GONE! BY NOW, YOUR FLAME SHOULD BE WORKING AT FULL STRENGTH!
GREAT, DOC! I WANNA SHOW MY PARTNERS IN THE FANTASTIC FOUR THAT I CAN TACKLE DR. OCTOPUS ALONE!
FLAME ON!
AND NOW, FOR--
RELAX, TORCH! DR. OCTOPUS HAS BEEN CAPTURED ALREADY!
THANKS TO YOU, TORCH, OCTOPUS IS SAFELY UNDER WRAPS! AND I OWE YOU ADDITIONAL THANKS BECAUSE, IF NOT FOR YOU, SPIDER-MAN MIGHT'VE BEEN FINISHED, TOO!
HUH?
SO LONG, TORCH! SEE YA AROUND, PAL!
FLAMIN' FIREBALLS! I DON'T GET IT! WHAT DID I DO??
THE NEXT DAY, THE HUMAN TORCH GIVES A PULSE-POUNDING DEMONSTRATION OF HIS FULL POWERS BEFORE RETURNING TO HIS HEADQUARTERS...
WISH SPIDER-MAN WAS STILL AROUND TO JOIN ME IN THIS SHOW! BUT I DON'T KNOW WHERE HE CUT OUT TO!
NOW THERE'S MY IDEA OF A HERO! THE HUMAN TORCH-- AND A GUY LIKE SPIDER-MAN, TOO! WHY DON'TCHA WATCH AND SEE WHAT A REAL MAN IS LIKE, BOOKWORM?
SOMEDAY I'LL TELL YOU WHY, LOUD MOUTH! AND I'M SURE GONNA ENJOY IT! YES SIR, IT'S GONNA BE A REAL PLEASURE!
AND, FOR THE FIRST TIME, A CASE ENDS WITHOUT PETER PARKER DELIVERING ANY PHOTOS TO MR. JAMESON! BUT, RIGHT NOW, PETER COULDN'T CARE LESS!
The END

HOT TIMES

Showing no lights, the helicopter settled down slowly to hover above the roof of the Nebel Building in New York's 42nd Street. A rope ladder dropped swiftly from the machine's side-door, and a darkly-dressed man with a heavy back-pack descended hurriedly, jumping the last few feet. The helicopter rose once more, and soon all trace of it was lost against the star-filled sky, save for the distant drone of its whirling rotors.

The man crossed to a small housing on the roof-top, in which was an access door leading to the floors below. He tried the door-handle, but muscular as he was, it failed to move. A slight smile creased his hard, lined face; what could be seen of it below the dark goggles which covered his eyes. It was as he had expected. A number of dealers in precious stones had offices on the floors below, and it was unlikely that the roof door would be left open, even if callers were not expected from this direction.

Pulling the covering from his back-pack, the man revealed two large metal cylinders strapped between his shoulders. Reaching behind him to open a valve, the man raised a strange looking blow-torch toward the door, ignited it, and began to burn away the lock. Long before he had completed the task, a loud electronic alarm began to wail through the still night air.

Smiling to himself once more, the man extinguished his torch and stepped away from the door, showing no further interest in it. The alarm continued as he zipped up a battered old leather jacket, then pushed up his goggles onto a forehead covered by an ancient leather flying helmet. He walked away to the edge of the roof and looked down over the parapet at the street, thirty floors below.

Now he'd see what developed . . .

Developments were not long in coming. Making his nightly patrol as Spider-man, Peter Parker's sensitive ears picked up the sound of the alarm from more than four blocks away. Swinging over the roof-tops, he started toward it immediately, debating with himself as to whether it would turn out to be another wild goose-chase. Knowing his luck, it had to be a false alarm; nothing else had been happening that night, and all he'd managed to do so far was expend an awful lot of energy for nothing.

Scuttling to the top of the building across the street, he saw the man still standing there casually, almost as if he was doing nothing more extraordinary than waiting for a passing bus. Or a passing Spider-man.

"Well then, fella . . ." muttered Spidey under his breath as he set up his camera, wait no longer!" And with that he launched himself toward the Nebel Building, trailing a line of webbing behind him.

Even as Spidey dropped toward the roof, the man pulled a pair of goggles over his eyes, and fiddled with something in his hand. An instant later, a jet of flame shot out through the air.

And neatly severed Spidey's web-line, a few feet above his head. The street below suddenly started to look a long way off.

But, recovering from his surprise in an instant, the web-spinner hurriedly flipped himself through the air even as he started to fall, and shot out another line. This time toward the Nebel Building itself. The line caught the parapet, held, and snapped taut, jerking Spidey to a halt a couple of storeys below the roof. With only his fingers and toes in contact with the wall, he scrambled up toward the parapet.

The man was still waiting for him when he reached the roof-top, a curious figure in his World War One flying leathers, a small flame still licking round the nozzle in his hand.

"Okay, friend, you've got a few questions to answer . . ." said Spidey, sizing up his opponent warily. "We'll start off with who are you, and what the heck do you think you're playing at . . .?"

The man merely grinned. The alarm continued to wail.

"Well, come on," prompted the web-spinner, moving forward cautiously. "They'll throw you out of the Super-villain's Guild if you don't have some sort of corny name. The Fire-bug? Terror-torch? The Blazer?"

"My name's Lance Taylor, heating engineer," came the reply. "But if you really need something better . . . my friends sometimes call me 'Thermic Lance . . !"

"After the stunt you just pulled, I don't think I'm going to be your friend," Spidey told him. "What's the game?"

'Some of my friends have hired me to kill you," Taylor told him, and at the same time another jet of flame shot across the roof-top.

Spidey hurled himself aside just in time, only to find the trail of fire following him as he moved. He leaped again, bounding and bouncing across the roof, the flames only inches behind him, until finally he found cover behind the door-housing.

"How about we *talk* about this?" he called, sticking his head round the corner of the wall. Another jet of flame was the only answer. "No need to get so hot-tempered!" he responded, drawing back hurriedly.

The alarm made it impossible to hear any foot-steps, but he could guess that Taylor was walking round the roof looking for a better angle. He moved back, then realised that was pointless. They could chase each other round the door-housing all night without getting anywhere . . . unless Taylor managed to fry him in the meantime.

But there was still a chance of catching the man off guard, and Spidey leaped up on top of the housing suddenly. Before Taylor spotted him, Spidey's web-shooters were in action. With dead aim, he put a thick glob of webbing over the nozzle of the flame-thrower.

Taylor burned through it in one and a half seconds flat. Spidey leaped back down to the roof. It looked like it was back to chasing each other round and round . . .

But that wouldn't get him anywhere. There seemed to be only two alternatives: run away, or carry the attack to his foe once more. And running away didn't fit in with his plans for the evening . . .

Webbing gushed forth from his wrist-shooters, and he wove it together into a globe about the size of a basket-ball. Then he paused, reaching out with his spider-sense. Taylor seemed to be coming round the door-housing from the left. Spidey went right, hoping to come round behind him.

But Taylor was being careful, keeping an eye out both ways, and he began to turn toward his foe as soon as he saw him, the flame-thrower rising.

"Taylor!" yelled Spider-man, and hurled the webbing globe straight at his opponent's head. Startled, Taylor pointed his weapon up and sprayed the globe with flames; but in the instant that his attention was diverted, Spidey was hurling himself forward in a low dive. He caught Taylor round the ankles and brought him down, flailing his fist into the man's stomach even as he fell.

But Taylor was fast, rolling aside shooting flame in all directions. Spidey felt the heat next to his shoulder and hurled himself away, and by the time he'd regained his feet, Taylor was scrambling to his feet.

But now there was a pause as Taylor checked a dial on his flame-thrower, then reached behind to the tanks on his back. A moment later there was a jet of fire from a nozzle below the tanks, and before Spidey could do anything to stop him, he rocketed straight up into the air.

"Another time, Spider-man!" Taylor yelled as he rose. Above the sound of the alarm, Spidey could hear the whir of a descending helicopter. He shook his head in wonderment. Not only did the

tanks provide fuel for the flame-thrower, they doubled as a jet-pack. Moments later, Taylor rendezvoused with the helicopter in mid-air. The flames died, and man and machine together whirred away into the dark night.

There was nothing Spidey could do except collect his camera and continue on his way.

There was no sign of Taylor the next night. Peter Parker had sold his photos to the *Daily Globe* as usual, and got a good front-page spread out of it; even if he was disgusted by the headline which read "Spider-man fought to a stand-still!"

But he was even more appalled by the news-item in the following day's paper. Lance Taylor had phoned the *Globe* to issue a challenge to Spider-man. He'd take him on in Central Park at ten o'clock that evening.

It wasn't the prospect of fighting the man that worried him, although that would be dangerous enough. He had to be there, or J. Jonah Jameson would have a field-day in the pages of the *Daily Globe;* but by announcing the time and place of the confrontation, Taylor had virtually guaranteed that there'd be a huge crowd of onlookers, police and press-men. And with Taylor slinging fire everywhere someone was bound to get hurt.

All of Spider-man's worst fears were confirmed when he arrived at the designated area in Central Park, keeping to the shadows and swinging through the tree-tops to make sure he wasn't seen. It was ten minutes before the hour, and a vast crowd had gathered expectantly. There was a carnival atmosphere, with men selling hot-dogs and cans of beer, souvenir posters of Spider-man, comic books . . . everything. There were vast numbers of police, as well.

But as a distant clock struck ten o'clock, there was no sign of Lance Taylor. For a moment, Spidey thought the man had chickened out of the contest, but then suddenly a tree burst into flame . . . at the far end of the park.

Taylor had turned up after all, but obviously he'd had the same ideas about the crowd as the web-spinner. Now Spidey dashed off through the trees as fast as his web-lines could carry him. If he could get to Taylor ahead of the crowds, he might be able to get this over with before any innocent bystanders got hurt.

He found Taylor not far from the burning tree, standing in a clearing. All around was a ring of trees, and as Spidey dropped down into the area, Taylor laughed.

"Our arena, Spider-man!" he announced, and suddenly all the surrounding trees burst into flame. Spidey looked round sourly. Taylor might not have given himself a crazy name, but he was just as much a showman as any of the other villains Spidey had fought. There was one advantage, though; the circle of fire would keep the crowds a safe distance away. The disadvantage was that now there'd be no overhanging branches for Spidey to hang a line on. The duel would have to be fought on foot.

He decided to go on the attack straight away, spraying a fine net of webbing into the air above Taylor's head, which should have fallen down to cover the man. But Taylor had already raised his flame-thrower and burned the web away before it got anywhere near him. Spidey followed up with a line toward his waist, but Taylor's reactions were fast, and that too vanished in a jet of fire.

A jet of fire which now swung toward Spider-man himself, as Taylor took his turn to attack. The web-spinner leaped fifteen feet in the air to avoid the flames, only to find himself in more trouble as soon as he landed. Fast as he moved, Taylor only had to stand in the middle of the burning ring of trees, turning his flame-thrower to follow Spidey's movements.

"Why don't you just give up, Spider-man!" shouted Taylor. "The mob have paid me a great deal of money to get rid of you, and I don't intend to fail this time . . !"

"Then they've wasted their money!" Spidey replied, suddenly hurling half a dozen small balls of webbing at his foe. Taylor burned three of them before they got near him; two missed; but one hit his hip and stuck there. Without thinking, he tried to brush it off with his free hand . . . only to find his hand stuck to his hip as well.

It was a problem which only took him a few seconds to sort out, narrowing the nozzle of his flame-thrower to produce a fine jet of flame with which he burned away the ball. But in those few seconds Spidey was leaping in, webbing Taylor's feet to the ground as he came, then bunching his fist for the knockout blow that would finish the contest.

But Taylor saw him just in time, twisting and ducking as best he could, and the blow glanced off his shoulder. He went sprawling, but by the time Spidey had recovered himself enough for another punch the flame-thrower was up and spraying death in his direction. Gritting his teeth with frustration, Spidey leaped away once more.

Taylor kept driving him back with more jets of flame until, with his foe twenty yards away, he had time to burn through the webbing about his feet and free himself. But as he scrambled upright, Spidey was leaping through the air again, twenty feet above his head. And as he passed over, another line of web shot down, blocking the nozzle of the flame-thrower. The web-spinner knew that would only hold up his foe temporarily, but the second line he cast was more effective. Taylor suddenly found both flame-thrower and the hand that held it webbed to his side.

By the time Spidey landed and turned toward his opponent, Taylor had managed to blast the webbing from the nozzle of his flame-thrower, but with his hand stuck to his hip, there was little he could do with it. He managed to twist round enough to divert Spidey's first attack with a low jet of fire, but unless he could find some way round the problem, it would only be a matter of time before the web-spinner had him.

Instead, Taylor decided to cut and run. As Spidey started forward again, he saw his foe reach behind his back with his free hand, and before there was time to get a web-line on him, Taylor was rocketing into the air once more.

"You're wasting your time, Taylor!" Spidey yelled, although he had no idea whether the man could hear him or not. "I phoned the cops and warned them about your little trick. The only 'copters you'll find up there are police ones . . . chasing everything else out of the sky over Central Park!"

Whether he'd heard or not, Taylor soon found the sky above was empty, and Spidey watched as the flame-trail from his jet-pack turned from going straight up to level with the ground. And as soon as he'd seen which direction his opponent was going in, Spidey was off in pursuit, leaping through a gap between the burning trees.

The fight had lasted barely a minute, but already the leading members of the crowd were streaming toward the burning trees. There were howls of disappointment as Spidey bounded over their heads, but he hadn't asked them to be there in the first place. Then he was out of the park and back on the streets of New York.

Swinging from building to building, leaping from roof-top to roof-top as fast as he could, Spidey managed to keep Taylor's flame-trail in sight, though there was no way he could keep up. But then Taylor stopped, hanging in mid-air for a moment. He seemed to hesitate, then cut off in a different direction, more or less at right angles to his previous course. It took the web-spinner a few seconds to realise why.

If Taylor had continued in the same direction, he would have found himself heading out over the river, and he obviously didn't have enough fuel left to make the crossing. Instead, he was moving along the shore and Spidey realised that if he cut across town at an angle, he'd be able to narrow the distance.

By the time the web-spinner was approaching the river shore, Taylor was already dropping from the sky, obviously looking for a landing space before his fuel ran out completely. Spidey decided to help him down.

A web-line shot up and curled round Taylor's ankle, and then Spidey was pulling him down out of the sky; while at the same time leaping forward to the very edge of the river bank. He had a pretty good idea of how he wanted to extinguish his fiery foe, and by deft manoeuvring he managed to pull Taylor down just where he wanted him.

Straight into the cool dark waters of the river.

The flame jets died in a spray of steam, but then there was a thrashing and splashing in the water.

"*Help*!" yelled Taylor. "I can't swim!"

Spidey couldn't believe it at first, but then he shrugged his shoulders wearily. Just his luck. The guy nearly burns him to death, and then he has to get soaked to save him. But there was nothing else for it.

Spidey dived into the river and swam strongly toward Taylor. The man was still thrashing wildly as the web-spinner reached him, and there was only one way to get him under control. It was hardly the punch he would liked to have given him, but Spidey tapped him gently on the jaw and knocked him unconscious.

Moments later, he had Taylor up on the bank, and was proceeding to web him tightly to a bollard when a police car drew up.

"Is that the fire maniac?" asked the officer, running toward him.

"It was . . ." remarked Spidey, shaking the water from his costume before leaping toward a nearby building. "He's more of a *damp squid* now!"

And with that, the web-spinner was gone into the darkness.

This, folks, is a
SILO-JIG!
Just trace off the shapes on to thin card, cut out and put together to make my silhouette.
Don't forget to mark the backs or it will take longer to get me together!

Spider-man's Simplistics

CAN YOU ARRANGE THE NUMBERS 1 TO 9 IN THE SQUARES BELOW SO THAT THE TOTAL OF EACH LINE– HORIZONTAL – VERTICAL AND DIAGONAL IS 15?

A.

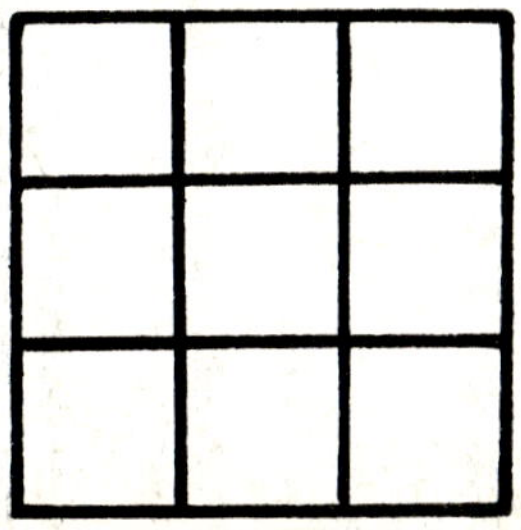

B.

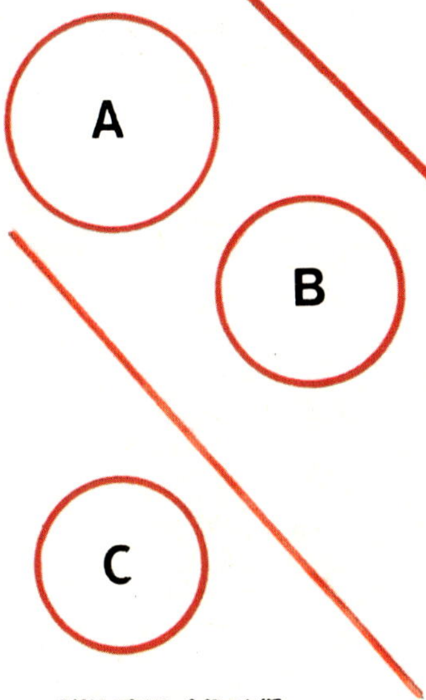

SEE THE ABOVE CIRCLES AND LINE– WELL, THE CIRCUMFERENCE OF ONE OF THESE CIRCLES IS EQUAL TO THE LENGTH OF THE LINE. WHICH? TRY YOUR EYE.

C. TRY THESE FOR SIZE.

1. IS A ZEBRA BLACK WITH WHITE STRIPES OR WHITE WITH BLACK STRIPES?
2. CAN YOU THINK OF A BIRD WHICH CAN FLY BACKWARDS?
3. WHICH FRUIT HAS ITS SEEDS ON THE OUTSIDE? COULD HAVE SOMETHING TO DO WITH THE CREAM.

D.

HERE'S A TRICK YOU CAN TRY. PLACE SIX GLASSES ON THE TABLE AS BELOW—ONE EMPTY THEN ONE HALF FULL AND SO ON:–

NOW ASK SOMEONE TO REARRANGE THEM SO THAT THERE ARE THREE EMPTY GLASSES TO ONE END AND THREE HALF-FULL TO THE OTHER — BUT YOU MUST MOVE ONLY ONE GLASS.

ANSWERS:–

A. 492–357 816. **B.** CIRCLE B.
C. 1. A ZEBRA IS WHITE WITH BLACK STRIPES
2. THE HUMMINGBIRD.
3. A STRAWBERRY. THE OUTSIDE IS COVERED WITH SEEDS.
D. TAKE GLASS 2. AND EMPTY IT INTO 5. THEN RETURN IT.

Hammer-Fist And Knife-Slice

A long fine blade snicked out from the heavy gauntlet on the thin man's hand, glinting in the street-lights. He glanced briefly at the edge, admiring his own handiwork, a foot long and sharper than a razor blade, and then slipped the knife through the crack in the door. He ran it up the inside of the door-frame until he found what he was looking for near the top corner, made a brief sawing movement, then stepped back, smiling.

"The alarm wire's cut," he announced to his bulky companion, then glanced up the street. There was still no sign of police or passers-by. "So now you may as well open the door . . ."

The larger man smirked and raised his gigantic fists, a slight electric whirring seeming to emanate from somewhere near his arm-pits. His fists, each encased in a dark velvet glove, and each almost as big as his own head, rose to his shoulders, then pounded forward against the door.

His first punch tore the door from its upper hinge with a cracking of wood and a wrenching of metal. His second, slightly misplaced, shattered the doorframe and took three bricks out of the surrounding wall besides. His third, no more than a gentle tap by comparison, laid the door flat on the ground.

The two men stood admiring their handiwork for a moment. The Boulnois Art Gallery stood wide open before them. Then, leaving his companion on watch outside, the thin small man stepped hurriedly within. One minute later, he had cut the canvases of three Dutch Old Masters from their frames. The blade slipped back into his gauntlet to lie along his forearm, and then he rolled the pictures up carefully and placed them in a long steel tube that hung over his shoulder.

Returning outside, he found the street was still empty. He and his companion crossed the street to a shadowed alley, and disappeared into the night.

The first police car arrived three minutes later, brought to the scene by a silent alarm from within the gallery. The officers switched off their siren and got out, staring in astonishment at the devastation. Then, while officer Edwards moved into the gallery to see what was missing, his companion, Heissig, made a brief radio report before stepping forward to examine the door.

And three minutes after that, Spider-man appeared, squatting atop a street light and surveying the scene.

"I heard your siren and thought I'd see what was happening," remarked the web-spinner. Heissig looked up at him sourly.

"You're a bit late," he said. "It's already happened . . ."

"Pictures?" asked Spidey, as Edwards emerged from the building.

"Three," said Edwards. "I guess we'll have to wait until the owner gets here to find out what they were. Professional job, though . . . very neatly cut from their frames . . ."

"And the alarm was neatly cut too," said Heissig. "Then it looks like they just smashed their way in. Must have been pretty powerful . . ."

"And I hear tell that *you're* pretty powerful . . ." said Edwards, looking up at the web-spinner, while his hand strayed near the holster at his hip.

"Don't look at me!" said Spidey. "I've got the perfect alibi. You just ask Patrolman Jones on 18th street. I was webbing up a mugger over there a few minutes ago. Came straight here from there . . ."

"Maybe you ought to come down to the precinct and answer a few questions anyway," Edwards said, but Spidey shook his head.

"Thought I'd have an early night," he told the policeman. "Besides the coffee down at your place tastes awful . . ."

And with that he leaped up to a nearby wall, and scuttled off into the darkness.

Perhaps it was Edwards' suspicions, or perhaps there was just something about the robbery that intrigued him, but Spidey decided he wanted to get whoever was responsible out of the way as soon as possible, so the next night found him on watch in the same area, patrolling back and forth. There was no reason to think they'd strike again so soon, but somehow he had a hunch that it was worth hanging around.

Whether his hunch was right or not, his spider-senses began to tingle about eight o'clock, and he immediately began to swing across the roof-tops in the direction indicated. At least there'd be some action tonight. He perched on a parapet and looked down at the street below.

The action was already starting, even as he set up his camera, lowering it on a web-line to get it closer to the scene. In the middle of the street stood a bulky man, waving down an armoured security truck, which had no alternative but to stop, short of running him down. The man was well over six and a half feet tall, and looked half as wide. He was normally dressed, but his fore-arms bulked hugely, and his gloved fists were the size of melons.

As the armoured truck came to a halt, the big man pounded one of those massive fists into the front of it. To Spidey's astonishment, he saw the fist

smash through the radiator grille, then carry straight on until the man's arm had sunk into the engine up to the elbow. The motor died instantly. Shrapnel from the shattered engine cut into the truck's tyres, and the nose settled down to the street with a tired wheezing noise.

Even as Spidey launched himself from the roof-top, the big man moved round to the rear of the truck and smashed open the armoured rear-door. Before the guards had time to react, a small ferret-like man dashed out from the side of the street. Two long blades shot out of his gauntlets and he thrust them toward the stunned guards' faces.

"And now," the thin man said. "If you'd kindly hand over the sapphires you're carrying, we'll be on our way . . ."

"Forget it, boys!" said Spidey, landing in the street behind them. "Playtime's over!"

With unruffled casualness, the two men turned to face the web-spinner.

"Ah, Spider-man," said the smaller of the two, smiling and bowing slightly. "We had a feeling we might run into you at some point. Well, no matter. Permit me to make the introductions. This large gentleman at my side is known as 'Hammer-fist'. I myself, insignificant as I am by comparison, am known as 'Knife-slice'. We are, as you'll gather, a team . . ."

"You're a pair of corn-balls . . ." Spidey told them.

"Perhaps so," responded Knife-slice, stepping forward and raising his wicked-looking blades threateningly. "You, however, will soon be . . . *corned beef!"*

"No way!" Spidey told him. "You're the guys who are going to get *canned!"*

But Knife-slice was already leaping forward to the attack. Spidey shot out a net of webbing, then stopped to stare in astonishment as the small man slit through it and tossed it aside. If his knives were *that* sharp . . .

A faint whirring like electric motors came from one side, and Spidey realised he'd been too astonished to pay much attention to what the big man was doing. Now he threw himself aside hurriedly as a gigantic fist looped down over his shoulder. It missed him by inches, but the fist carried on down and smashed into the surface of the road. When Spidey glanced back, he saw a crater in the tarmac a foot wide and six inches deep.

"Don't you think there are enough pot-holes in the roads around here already?" he joked, but the humour was brittle. This was obviously the guy who had smashed his way into the Boulnois gallery the night before. And with power like that in his fists . . .

Except they weren't real fists, he realised, looking at the bulky forearms and listening to the whir of the motors. Obviously he had casings of heavy steel several inches thick drawn over his hands like gloves, and a powered exo-skeleton extending up his arms to enable him to move them. It was quite an engineering feat, the web-spinner had to admit. But admiring his foes didn't get them defeated.

He shot forth a line of webbing toward the big man, but by now his smaller companion had moved closer to his side. True to his name, Knife-slice slashed through the webbing before it entangled anything. It looked like he'd have to try get in close and slug it out.

Behind his foes, he could see the security guards scrambling to gather up the bags of jewels inside the truck. The men ran off hurriedly down the street before the crooks noticed them. Well, if nothing else, the web-spinner had managed to foil the robbery . . .

"Well, come along, Spider-man," taunted Knife-slice, eyes glinting like the edges of his blades. "The sooner we get this over, the sooner we can exault over the fallen hero!"

"You've got your head in the clouds, fella," Spidey said, moving closer. "Let's see if we can't keep your feet on the ground . . ."

And even as he spoke, Spidey shot forth a thick stream of sticky webbing. Knife-slice did his best to leap aside. But his best wasn't quite good enough, and he suddenly found one foot glued securely to the ground.

Then the web-spinner was hurling himself forward, feet first, He struck Hammer-fist squarely in the chest and sent the big man reeling backwards. He went down, his fists clanging as they hit the road. But as Spidey closed in, one of those fists swung up in a whistling arc in front of him. The web-spinner jumped back out of the way, and Hammer-fist was on his feet again in an instant.

Spidey raised his fists and moved in again. Like the young punk who dreams of knocking out the heavyweight champion of the world, he wanted to finish this with a punch . . . if the man was so proud of his fists, he wanted to show what he could do with his own.

But just as he got within punching range, his spider-senses tingled. Looking over his shoulder, he saw Knife-slice leaping toward him, one foot bare. Behind was his shoe, still neatly glued to the road.

Spidey dodged hurriedly as one of the blades whistled past his shoulder. Dodged straight into a mighty hammer blow from a massive steel fist.

The lights went out.

He had no idea how long he was unconscious. Probably not long, but long enough for a small crowd to gather and stare at him curiously. His jaw was aching hideously, but touching it gingerly he thought it wasn't broken. He'd probably have a headache for days though.

Two men started to push through the crowd, and he recognised officers Heissig and Edwards again. But he was in no mood for answering any questions. Getting to his feet shakily, he summoned all his energy and leaped to a nearby wall. Still trying to clear his head, he retrieved his camera and started slowly back toward his apartment.

Peter Parker woke late, and immediately found a difficult decision on his hands. Should he sell the pictures to the *Globe?* Yes, he wanted the money they'd bring, but he could imagine how Jameson would play the story. Still, the rent was about due, and maybe he could persuade them to play it as "Spider-man foils robbery".

Later that day, he knew he'd made the wrong decision. There were his pictures on the front page alright, but the headline, several inches high, screamed *"Spider-man defeated!"*

Well, that only made it more urgent to get Messrs. Hammer-fist and Knife-slice behind bars as soon as possible. And there was one small lead that he might be able to follow up. Assuming that his opponents had built their own equipment, they obviously had to have a knowledge of engineering, and the facilities to put the stuff together. Peter started going through the classified phone directory, looking for engineering companies in that area of New York.

He ended up with a list of six establishments, which didn't seem to help much, as his men could be working in any of them. But as he looked at the list again, a new idea struck him. Only one of the companies was actually a partnership. Eberhard and Fairservis Inc. Well, maybe he'd pay them a visit that night. If his jaw held together . . .

The moon shone down full on the small yard beside Eberhard and Fairservis's workshop. And on the roof of that same establishment, Spider-man surveyed the scene. Opposite him rose a tall building with a steel fire-escape running up the outside. To his right, a small factory backed onto the yard, to the left was a wall and gateway that led into the street. And below him, two figures emerged from the engineering shop.

One was a small man, quick of movement and already watchful. The other was large with massive fists. Spidey set his camera and dropped over the edge of the roof.

"Going somewhere, gents?" he inquired, landing lightly on the balls of his feet.

"He's found us!" exclaimed Hammer-fist, stunned.

"Stupid of you, Spider-man," said Knife-slice quickly. "Last night we were prepared to leave you in the street. This time, though, you'll have to *die . . ."*

"Aw, and I didn't even have time to write my will!" quipped Spidey, shooting a web-line between the two men. The line missed them both as they moved aside, but that was just what Spidey wanted. His first task was to separate them, and he cast another line at Knife-slice's waist.

The line caught, and Spidey immediately began to swing the small man round. A second later, the sharp blade cut through the line, but by then Knife-slice was on the move; and as soon as the tension was released, he went hurtling away across the yard. And before he could recover, Spidey was leaping toward Hammer-fist.

The big man raised his hands ready to strike, but Spidey's next move took him by surprise. Bouncing eight feet in the air, the web-spinner caught hold of one of the massive fists as he passed overhead. Caught hold of it and wrenched. There was the sound of tearing metal, and a strangely high-pitched cry from the big man.

When Spidey landed, he held a large iron fist and a trailing skeletal arm in his hand. He looked back to see Hammer-fist standing there with one perfectly ordinary arm hanging limply by his side. He was whimpering with pain.

Knife-slice, meanwhile, had hit the wall after Spidey had flung him aside, and was still recovering his breath. The web-spinner moved fast toward Hammer-fist, eager to get the big man finished before his smaller companion could get back in the fray.

Hammer-fist saw him coming, but instead of putting up a fight, he began to scramble away, holding his one remaining machine-arm close to his side; obviously afraid of having that one torn off as well.

But that was all Spidey wanted. He grabbed the man by the shoulder, spun him round, and punched him heavily on the jaw. There was a very satisfying thud, and Hammer-fist hit the ground like a falling tree.

Knife-slice had started to come forward, but now stopped dead in his tracks. Spidey cast a net of webbing towards him, hoping to take him off guard, but the little man managed to get both of his blades up in time to cut it down. Then he broke and ran toward the fire-escape. Spidey watched him go, smiling under his mask.

The fire-escape extended up five floors, and the web-spinner let his quarry reach the fourth floor before making a move. One leap carried him to the third floor landing; another took him to the roof.

He was standing there casually when Knife-slice got to the top of the fire-escape, gasping for breath. The man's eyes bulged in surprise.

He raised his knives, but Spidey was too quick. From a range of only a couple of feet, the web-spinner cast two thin lines around the man's wrists, then quite deliberately kicked him over the edge of the fire-escape. The lines tautened after five or six feet, and Spidey tied them round the rail of the fire-escape. When he looked down, Knife-slice was dangling there in mid-air by his wrists.

"This won't stop me!" yelled Knife-slice. "I can cut through one line and climb up the other . . ."

"You could do," Spidey agreed. "But I wouldn't if I were you. Those lines are very thin, and it'll take two to support your weight. You cut through one, and . . . well, it's a long way to the ground!"

Knife-slice looked down five floors to the yard below, and shuddered. "I'll think of *something!*" he cried.

"Sure you will," chuckled Spidey. "You just have a good think while I go off and call the cops . . ."

Five minutes later, officers Edwards and Heissig came into the yard, looking in some surprise at Hammer-fist, still prone on the ground.

"Where's the other one?" asked Edwards. Spidey glanced upwards to where Knife-slice still dangled, as before.

"Oh, he's hanging around somewhere . . !"

Spider-man's Deadly Checkerboard Game!

Here's a thrilling game to play! Spidey has been trapped in the deserted Temple of Mathmas! His web power is useless and he must get to the doorway by way of the squares. But some of the red one's are deadly hazards! Two can play this game (or more if you double up on the squares!) All you need is a dice and counters!

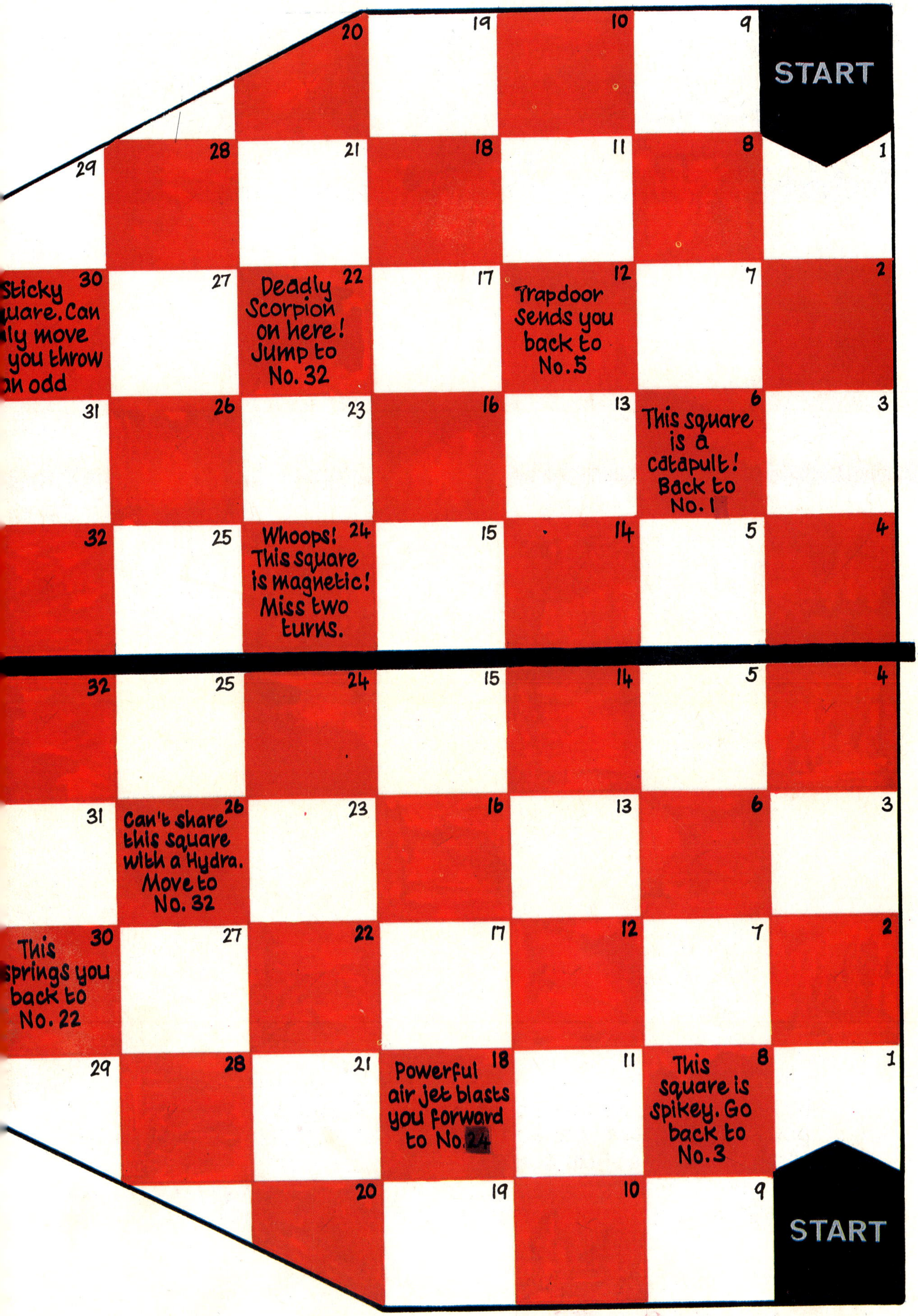
START
Sticky 30
uare. Can
ly move
you throw
n odd
Deadly Scorpion on here! Jump to No. 32 22
Trapdoor sends you back to No. 5 12
This square is a catapult! Back to No. 1 6
Whoops! This square is magnetic! Miss two turns. 24
Can't share this square with a Hydra. Move to No. 32 26
This springs you back to No. 22 30
Powerful air jet blasts you forward to No. 24 18
This square is spikey. Go back to No. 3 8
START

Stan Lee PRESENTS: SPIDER-MAN AND CAPTAIN AMERICA
TOM DeFALCO WRITER / HERB TRIMPE ARTIST / MIKE ESPOSITO INKER / DIANA ALBERS LETTERER / CARL GAFFORD COLORIST / DENNIS O'NEIL EDITOR / JIM SHOOTER EDITOR-IN-CHIEF
"A SAVAGE STING HAS-- THE SCORPION!"
MR. GARGAN--? CAN YOU HEAR ME, MR. GARGAN?
...GOTTA PAY! THAT STINKING, LOUSY NEWSPAPER PUBLISHER'S GOTTA PAY FOR MAKING ME INTO A MONSTER! I'M GONNA KILL J. JONAH JAMESON-- SLOW AND DIRTY!
SPIDER-MAN, TOO!
IT'S NO USE, DR. NOSEBLUM. HE'S LOST... IN HIS OWN PRIVATE UNIVERSE!

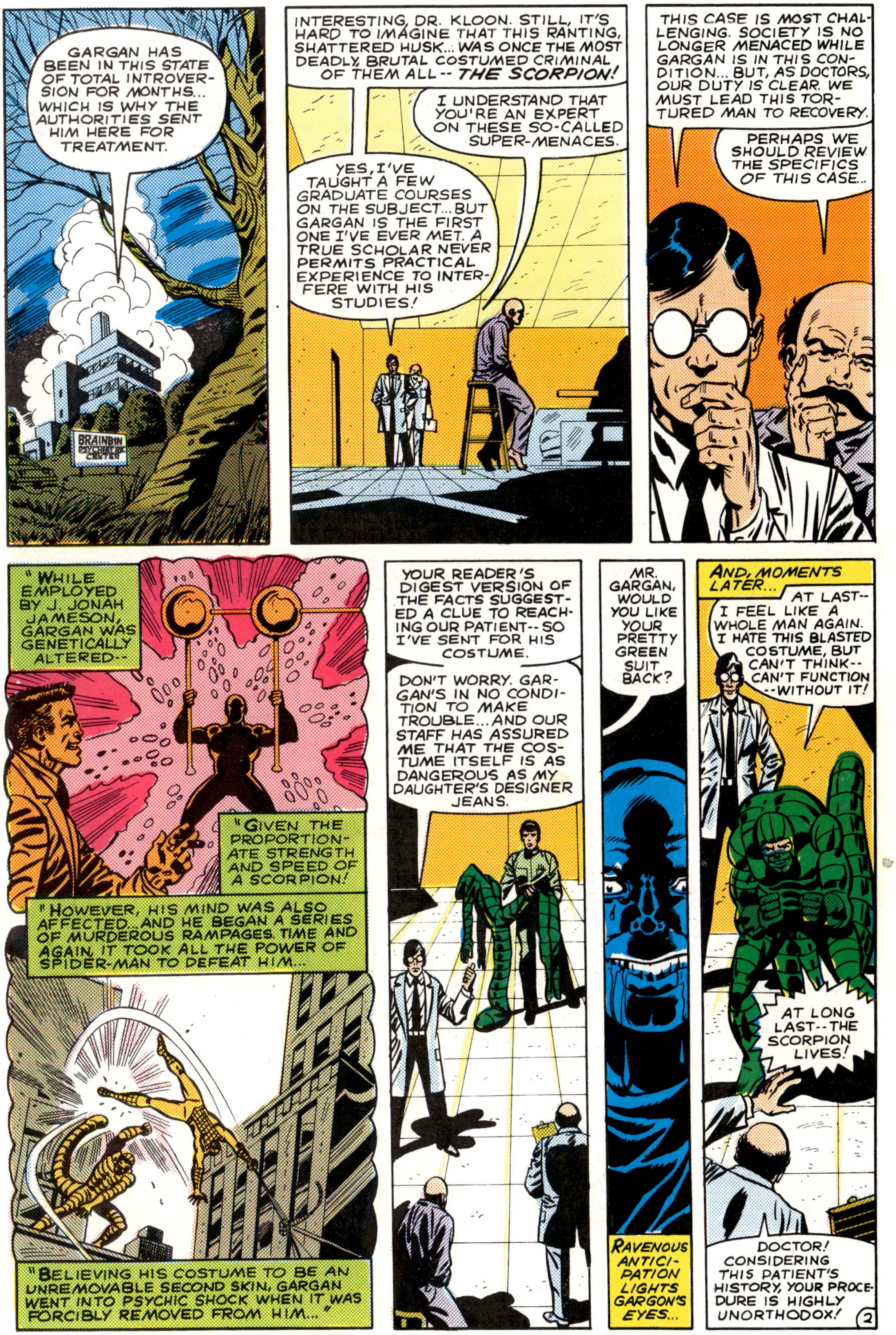
GARGAN HAS BEEN IN THIS STATE OF TOTAL INTROVERSION FOR MONTHS... WHICH IS WHY THE AUTHORITIES SENT HIM HERE FOR TREATMENT.
BRAINBIN PSYCHIATRIC CENTER
INTERESTING, DR. KLOON. STILL, IT'S HARD TO IMAGINE THAT THIS RANTING, SHATTERED HUSK... WAS ONCE THE MOST DEADLY, BRUTAL COSTUMED CRIMINAL OF THEM ALL -- THE SCORPION!
I UNDERSTAND THAT YOU'RE AN EXPERT ON THESE SO-CALLED SUPER-MENACES.
YES, I'VE TAUGHT A FEW GRADUATE COURSES ON THE SUBJECT... BUT GARGAN IS THE FIRST ONE I'VE EVER MET. A TRUE SCHOLAR NEVER PERMITS PRACTICAL EXPERIENCE TO INTERFERE WITH HIS STUDIES!
THIS CASE IS MOST CHALLENGING. SOCIETY IS NO LONGER MENACED WHILE GARGAN IS IN THIS CONDITION... BUT, AS DOCTORS, OUR DUTY IS CLEAR. WE MUST LEAD THIS TORTURED MAN TO RECOVERY.
PERHAPS WE SHOULD REVIEW THE SPECIFICS OF THIS CASE...
"WHILE EMPLOYED BY J. JONAH JAMESON, GARGAN WAS GENETICALLY ALTERED--
"GIVEN THE PROPORTIONATE STRENGTH AND SPEED OF A SCORPION!
"HOWEVER, HIS MIND WAS ALSO AFFECTED... AND HE BEGAN A SERIES OF MURDEROUS RAMPAGES. TIME AND AGAIN, IT TOOK ALL THE POWER OF SPIDER-MAN TO DEFEAT HIM...
"BELIEVING HIS COSTUME TO BE AN UNREMOVABLE SECOND SKIN, GARGAN WENT INTO PSYCHIC SHOCK WHEN IT WAS FORCIBLY REMOVED FROM HIM..."
YOUR READER'S DIGEST VERSION OF THE FACTS SUGGESTED A CLUE TO REACHING OUR PATIENT-- SO I'VE SENT FOR HIS COSTUME.
DON'T WORRY. GARGAN'S IN NO CONDITION TO MAKE TROUBLE... AND OUR STAFF HAS ASSURED ME THAT THE COSTUME ITSELF IS AS DANGEROUS AS MY DAUGHTER'S DESIGNER JEANS.
MR. GARGAN, WOULD YOU LIKE YOUR PRETTY GREEN SUIT BACK?
RAVENOUS ANTICIPATION LIGHTS GARGON'S EYES...
AND, MOMENTS LATER...
AT LAST-- I FEEL LIKE A WHOLE MAN AGAIN. I HATE THIS BLASTED COSTUME, BUT CAN'T THINK-- CAN'T FUNCTION --WITHOUT IT!
AT LONG LAST-- THE SCORPION LIVES!
DOCTOR! CONSIDERING THIS PATIENT'S HISTORY, YOUR PROCEDURE IS HIGHLY UNORTHODOX!
2

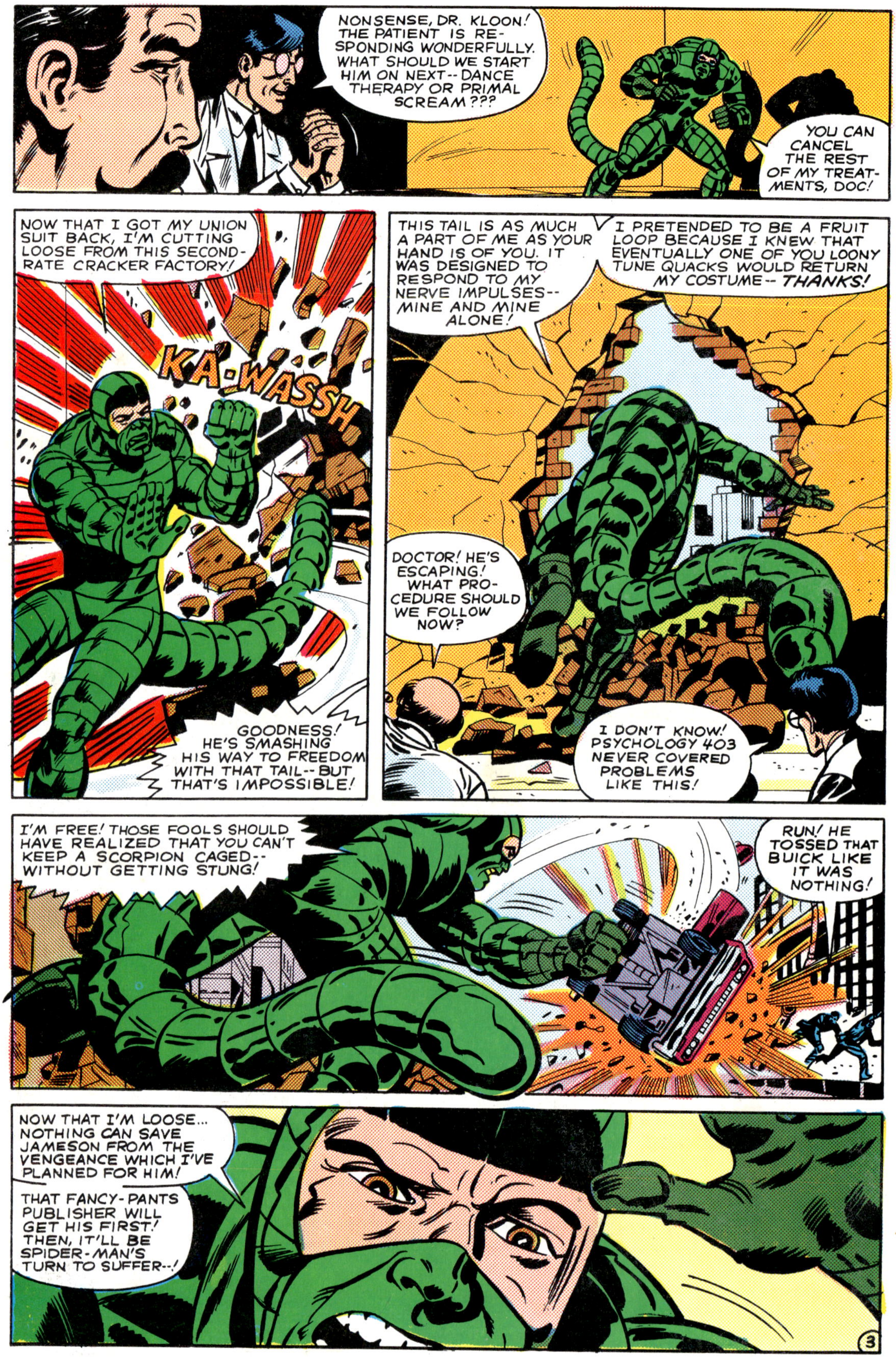
NONSENSE, DR. KLOON! THE PATIENT IS RESPONDING WONDERFULLY. WHAT SHOULD WE START HIM ON NEXT--DANCE THERAPY OR PRIMAL SCREAM???
YOU CAN CANCEL THE REST OF MY TREATMENTS, DOC!
NOW THAT I GOT MY UNION SUIT BACK, I'M CUTTING LOOSE FROM THIS SECOND-RATE CRACKER FACTORY!
KA-WASSH
GOODNESS! HE'S SMASHING HIS WAY TO FREEDOM WITH THAT TAIL--BUT THAT'S IMPOSSIBLE!
THIS TAIL IS AS MUCH A PART OF ME AS YOUR HAND IS OF YOU. IT WAS DESIGNED TO RESPOND TO MY NERVE IMPULSES--MINE AND MINE ALONE!
I PRETENDED TO BE A FRUIT LOOP BECAUSE I KNEW THAT EVENTUALLY ONE OF YOU LOONY TUNE QUACKS WOULD RETURN MY COSTUME--THANKS!
DOCTOR! HE'S ESCAPING! WHAT PROCEDURE SHOULD WE FOLLOW NOW?
I DON'T KNOW! PSYCHOLOGY 403 NEVER COVERED PROBLEMS LIKE THIS!
I'M FREE! THOSE FOOLS SHOULD HAVE REALIZED THAT YOU CAN'T KEEP A SCORPION CAGED--WITHOUT GETTING STUNG!
RUN! HE TOSSED THAT BUICK LIKE IT WAS NOTHING!
NOW THAT I'M LOOSE... NOTHING CAN SAVE JAMESON FROM THE VENGEANCE WHICH I'VE PLANNED FOR HIM!
THAT FANCY-PANTS PUBLISHER WILL GET HIS FIRST! THEN, IT'LL BE SPIDER-MAN'S TURN TO SUFFER--!
3

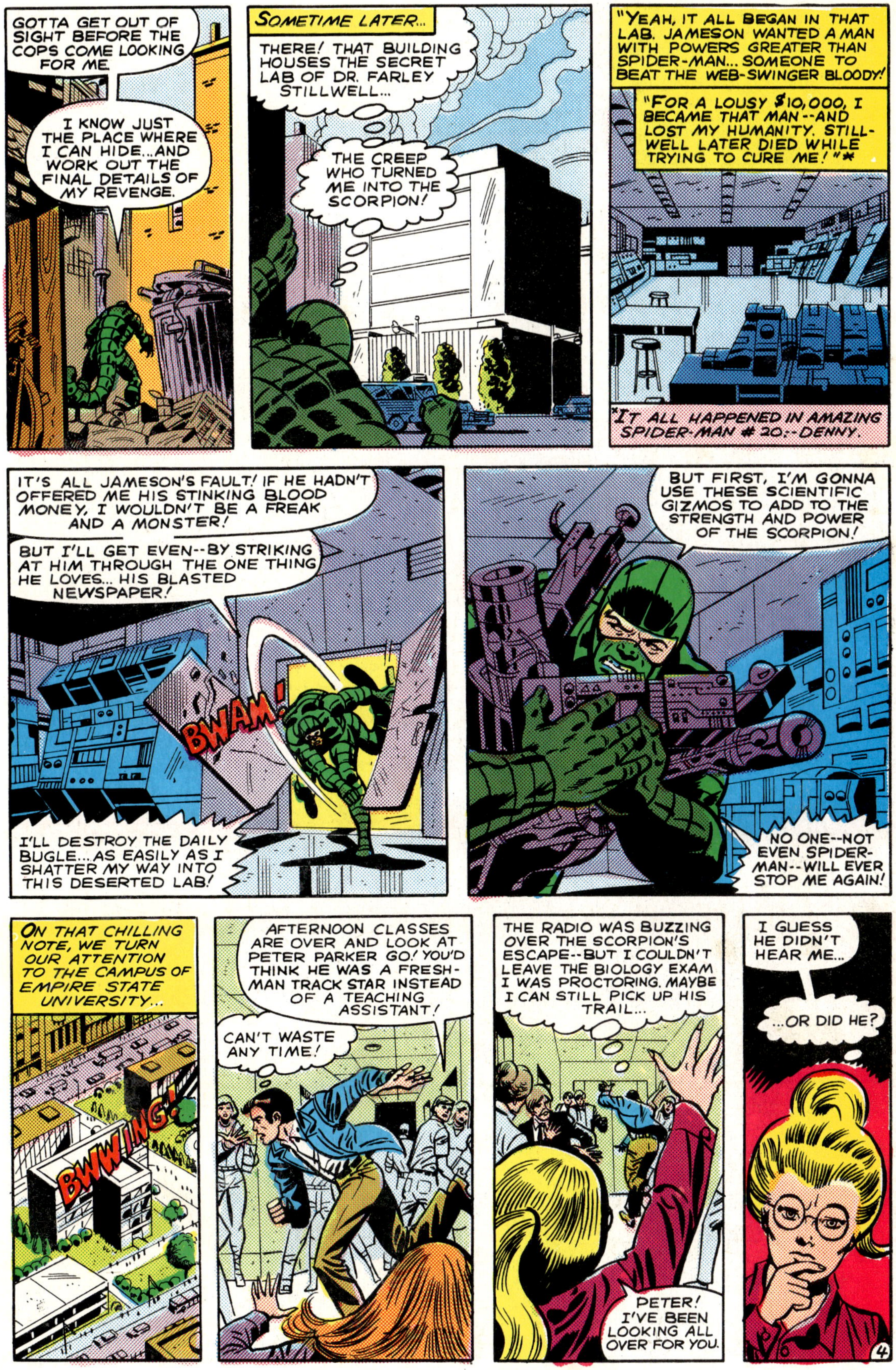

GOTTA GET OUT OF SIGHT BEFORE THE COPS COME LOOKING FOR ME.
I KNOW JUST THE PLACE WHERE I CAN HIDE...AND WORK OUT THE FINAL DETAILS OF MY REVENGE.
SOMETIME LATER...
THERE! THAT BUILDING HOUSES THE SECRET LAB OF DR. FARLEY STILLWELL...
THE CREEP WHO TURNED ME INTO THE SCORPION!
"YEAH, IT ALL BEGAN IN THAT LAB. JAMESON WANTED A MAN WITH POWERS GREATER THAN SPIDER-MAN... SOMEONE TO BEAT THE WEB-SWINGER BLOODY!
"FOR A LOUSY $10,000, I BECAME THAT MAN--AND LOST MY HUMANITY. STILLWELL LATER DIED WHILE TRYING TO CURE ME!"*
*IT ALL HAPPENED IN AMAZING SPIDER-MAN #20.-DENNY.
IT'S ALL JAMESON'S FAULT! IF HE HADN'T OFFERED ME HIS STINKING BLOOD MONEY, I WOULDN'T BE A FREAK AND A MONSTER!
BUT I'LL GET EVEN--BY STRIKING AT HIM THROUGH THE ONE THING HE LOVES... HIS BLASTED NEWSPAPER!
BWAM!
I'LL DESTROY THE DAILY BUGLE...AS EASILY AS I SHATTER MY WAY INTO THIS DESERTED LAB!
BUT FIRST, I'M GONNA USE THESE SCIENTIFIC GIZMOS TO ADD TO THE STRENGTH AND POWER OF THE SCORPION!
NO ONE--NOT EVEN SPIDER-MAN--WILL EVER STOP ME AGAIN!
ON THAT CHILLING NOTE, WE TURN OUR ATTENTION TO THE CAMPUS OF EMPIRE STATE UNIVERSITY...
BWWING!
AFTERNOON CLASSES ARE OVER AND LOOK AT PETER PARKER GO! YOU'D THINK HE WAS A FRESHMAN TRACK STAR INSTEAD OF A TEACHING ASSISTANT!
CAN'T WASTE ANY TIME!
THE RADIO WAS BUZZING OVER THE SCORPION'S ESCAPE--BUT I COULDN'T LEAVE THE BIOLOGY EXAM I WAS PROCTORING. MAYBE I CAN STILL PICK UP HIS TRAIL...
PETER! I'VE BEEN LOOKING ALL OVER FOR YOU.
I GUESS HE DIDN'T HEAR ME...
...OR DID HE?
4

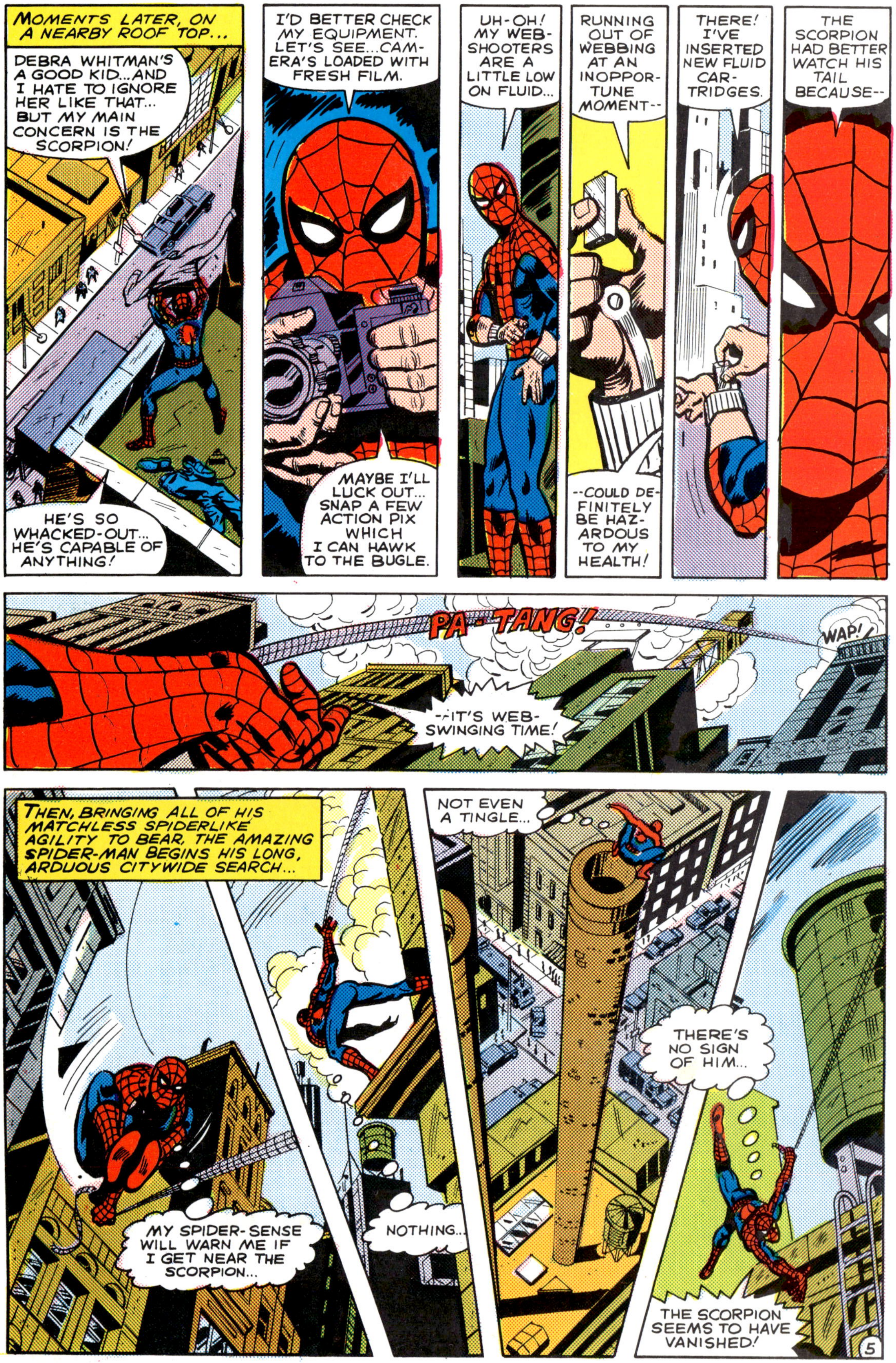

MOMENTS LATER, ON A NEARBY ROOF TOP...
DEBRA WHITMAN'S A GOOD KID...AND I HATE TO IGNORE HER LIKE THAT... BUT MY MAIN CONCERN IS THE SCORPION!
HE'S SO WHACKED-OUT... HE'S CAPABLE OF ANYTHING!
I'D BETTER CHECK MY EQUIPMENT. LET'S SEE...CAMERA'S LOADED WITH FRESH FILM.
MAYBE I'LL LUCK OUT... SNAP A FEW ACTION PIX WHICH I CAN HAWK TO THE BUGLE.
UH-OH! MY WEB-SHOOTERS ARE A LITTLE LOW ON FLUID...
RUNNING OUT OF WEBBING AT AN INOPPORTUNE MOMENT--
--COULD DEFINITELY BE HAZARDOUS TO MY HEALTH!
THERE! I'VE INSERTED NEW FLUID CARTRIDGES.
THE SCORPION HAD BETTER WATCH HIS TAIL BECAUSE--
PA-TANG!
WAP!
--IT'S WEB-SWINGING TIME!
THEN, BRINGING ALL OF HIS MATCHLESS SPIDERLIKE AGILITY TO BEAR, THE AMAZING SPIDER-MAN BEGINS HIS LONG, ARDUOUS CITYWIDE SEARCH...
MY SPIDER-SENSE WILL WARN ME IF I GET NEAR THE SCORPION...
NOTHING...
NOT EVEN A TINGLE...
THERE'S NO SIGN OF HIM...
THE SCORPION SEEMS TO HAVE VANISHED!
5

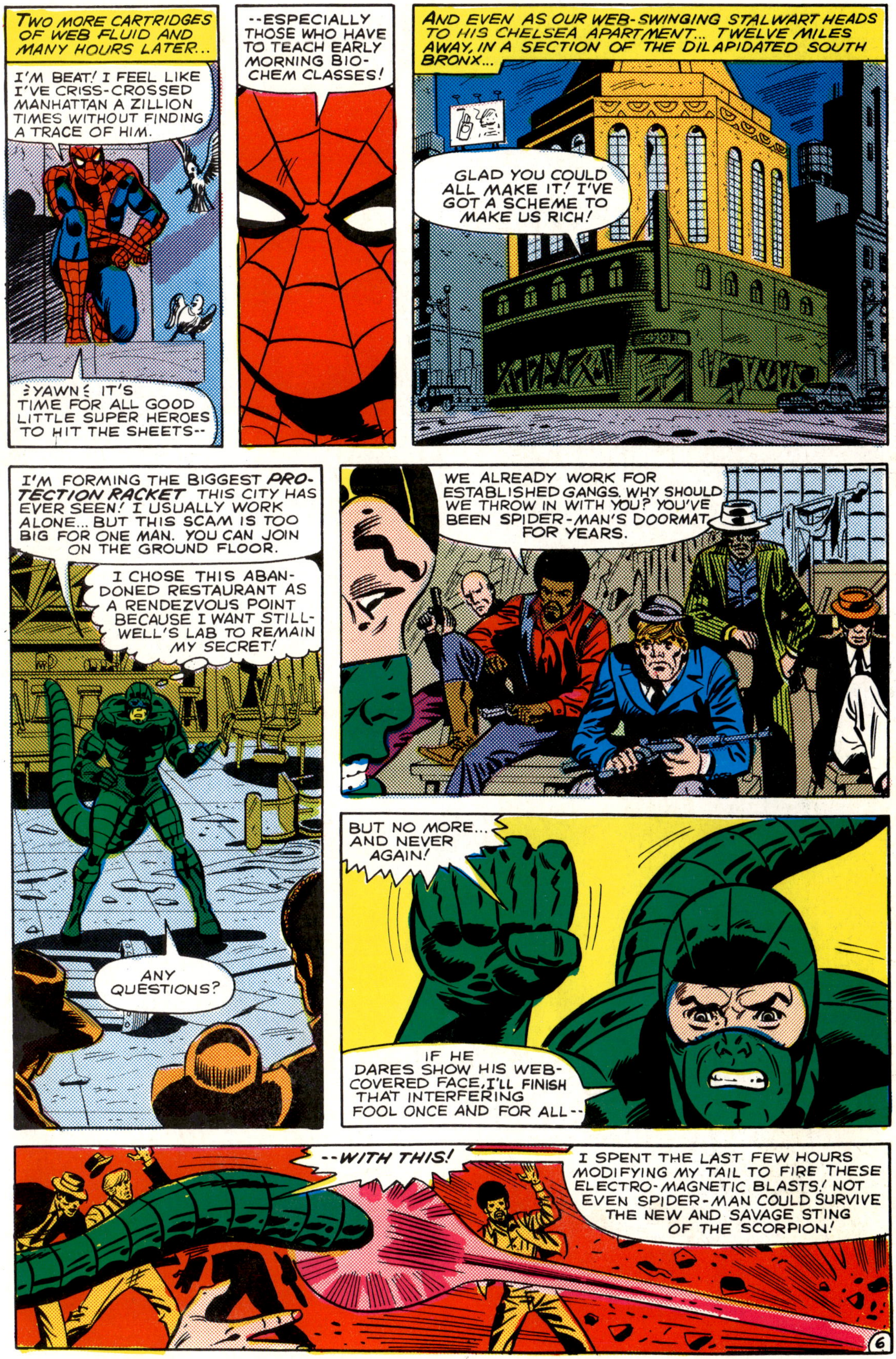
TWO MORE CARTRIDGES OF WEB FLUID AND MANY HOURS LATER...
I'M BEAT! I FEEL LIKE I'VE CRISS-CROSSED MANHATTAN A ZILLION TIMES WITHOUT FINDING A TRACE OF HIM.
≶YAWN≶ IT'S TIME FOR ALL GOOD LITTLE SUPER HEROES TO HIT THE SHEETS--
--ESPECIALLY THOSE WHO HAVE TO TEACH EARLY MORNING BIO-CHEM CLASSES!
AND EVEN AS OUR WEB-SWINGING STALWART HEADS TO HIS CHELSEA APARTMENT... TWELVE MILES AWAY, IN A SECTION OF THE DILAPIDATED SOUTH BRONX...
GLAD YOU COULD ALL MAKE IT! I'VE GOT A SCHEME TO MAKE US RICH!
I'M FORMING THE BIGGEST PROTECTION RACKET THIS CITY HAS EVER SEEN! I USUALLY WORK ALONE... BUT THIS SCAM IS TOO BIG FOR ONE MAN. YOU CAN JOIN ON THE GROUND FLOOR.
I CHOSE THIS ABANDONED RESTAURANT AS A RENDEZVOUS POINT BECAUSE I WANT STILLWELL'S LAB TO REMAIN MY SECRET!
ANY QUESTIONS?
WE ALREADY WORK FOR ESTABLISHED GANGS. WHY SHOULD WE THROW IN WITH YOU? YOU'VE BEEN SPIDER-MAN'S DOORMAT FOR YEARS.
BUT NO MORE... AND NEVER AGAIN!
IF HE DARES SHOW HIS WEB-COVERED FACE, I'LL FINISH THAT INTERFERING FOOL ONCE AND FOR ALL--
--WITH THIS!
I SPENT THE LAST FEW HOURS MODIFYING MY TAIL TO FIRE THESE ELECTRO-MAGNETIC BLASTS! NOT EVEN SPIDER-MAN COULD SURVIVE THE NEW AND SAVAGE STING OF THE SCORPION!
6

DULY IMPRESSED BY THE SCORPION'S DEADLY NEW WEAPON, THE HARDENED CRIMINALS QUICKLY SWEAR THEIR ALLEGIANCE, THEN...
OUR FIRST TARGET IS THE DAILY BUGLE! CONSIDER IT A FREE SAMPLE...ONCE WE DRIVE IT UNDER, THE CITY FATHERS WILL KNOW THAT WE MEAN BUSINESS...AND THEY'LL BE HOT FOR OUR PROTECTION!
AND I'LL HAVE MY REVENGE AGAINST JAMESON!
IN THE DAYS THAT FOLLOW, A CAREFULLY PLANNED CAMPAIGN OF TERROR ERUPTS WITHIN THE CITY...
UNDER THE SAVAGE LEADERSHIP OF THE SCORPION, RETAILERS WHO CARRY THE DAILY BUGLE ARE HARASSED!
WHOLESALE OUTLETS ARE RANSACKED AND LEFT IN RUINS!
INDEPENDENT DISTRIBUTORS ARE SABOTAGED!
FEARING LIKE REPRISALS, OTHER BUSINESS LEADERS QUICKLY CAPITULATE TO THE EXTORTION DEMANDS OF THE SCORPION!
DAILY
DAILY BUG
WHILE, IN THE OFFICE OF OUR FAVORITE NEWSPAPER PUBLISHER, J. JONAH JAMESON...
ROBERTSON! OUR CIRCULATION IS OFF BY 30%! THAT MANIAC IS OUT TO RUIN ME!
JONAH! MAYBE YOU SHOULD LEAVE TOWN.
HOW CAN I--WHILE MY PAPER'S IN DANGER??
WHY ME? WHY MUST THE GENTLE, THE GENEROUS ALWAYS SUFFER FROM LIFE'S BITTER ADVERSITIES?
TRY TO REMAIN CALM. THE POLICE WILL STOP HIM... EVENTUALLY.
OUR CASH RESERVES ARE TOO LOW TO SURVIVE A LONG SIEGE. I KNEW I SHOULDN'T HAVE GIVEN OUR STAFF THOSE $5 BONUSES FOR CHRISTMAS!
7

AND EVEN AS A LESS-THAN-JOLLY JAMESON CURSES A CRUEL AND UNCARING FATE...
THIS IS THE PLACE!
THE ONLY STORE IN A FIFTEEN BLOCK RADIUS THAT STILL SELLS THE BUGLE!
DAILY BUGLE SOLD HE
DANNY BOY! I THINK THE OWNER MAY BE HARD OF HEARING -- OR JUST PLAIN STUPID!
NO SWEAT, MANNO! I'M GOING TO DELIVER THE MESSAGE TO HIM PERSONALLY!
BUT...
HEY!!! SOMEONE'S STEALING MY CINDERBLOCK! BUT WHY--?
DO YOU KNOW ME-- OR DO I HAVE TO SHOW YOU AN AMERICAN EXPRESS CARD?
SPIDER-MAN!
THANK GOODNESS! MY CREDIT CARDS ARE IN MY OTHER COSTUME!
NOW THAT THE FORMAL INTRODUCTIONS ARE OVER... I BELIEVE THAT THIS PLAYTHING BELONGS TO YOU!
UFFF!
BWAF!
TEMPER! TEMPER! SWINGING WILDLY WITH THAT CROWBAR IS NOT THE ACCEPTED WAY OF MAKING SPIDEY-BURGERS--
--ESPECIALLY WHEN I CAN USE MY WEBBING TO SWING BEHIND YOU--
UNNNN
KWAK!
--AND DANCE ON THE BACK OF YOUR HEAD!
8

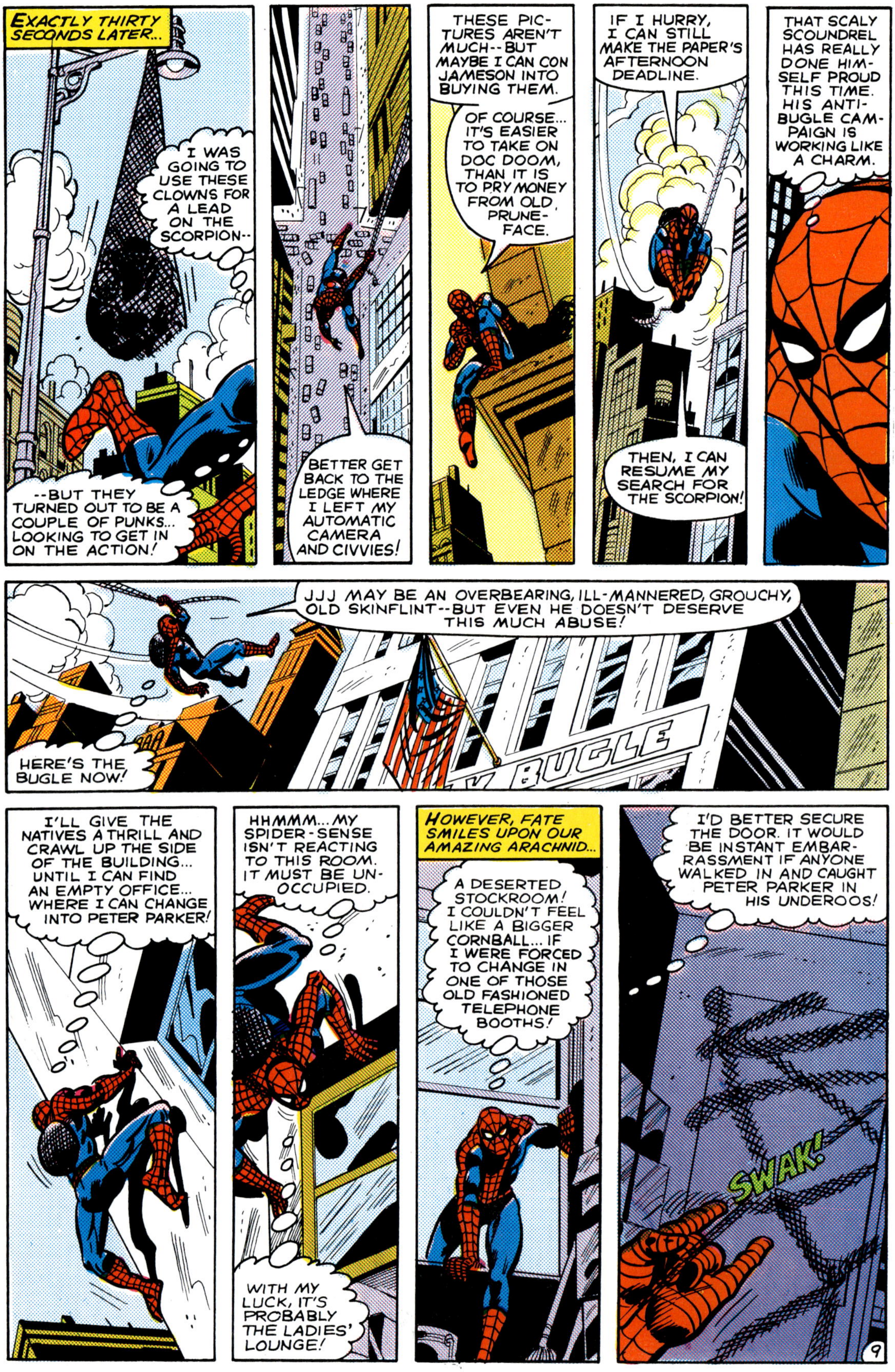
EXACTLY THIRTY SECONDS LATER...
I WAS GOING TO USE THESE CLOWNS FOR A LEAD ON THE SCORPION--
--BUT THEY TURNED OUT TO BE A COUPLE OF PUNKS... LOOKING TO GET IN ON THE ACTION!
BETTER GET BACK TO THE LEDGE WHERE I LEFT MY AUTOMATIC CAMERA AND CIVVIES!
THESE PICTURES AREN'T MUCH--BUT MAYBE I CAN CON JAMESON INTO BUYING THEM.
OF COURSE... IT'S EASIER TO TAKE ON DOC DOOM, THAN IT IS TO PRY MONEY FROM OLD PRUNE-FACE.
IF I HURRY, I CAN STILL MAKE THE PAPER'S AFTERNOON DEADLINE.
THEN, I CAN RESUME MY SEARCH FOR THE SCORPION!
THAT SCALY SCOUNDREL HAS REALLY DONE HIMSELF PROUD THIS TIME. HIS ANTI-BUGLE CAMPAIGN IS WORKING LIKE A CHARM.
JJJ MAY BE AN OVERBEARING, ILL-MANNERED, GROUCHY, OLD SKINFLINT--BUT EVEN HE DOESN'T DESERVE THIS MUCH ABUSE!
HERE'S THE BUGLE NOW!
BUGLE
I'LL GIVE THE NATIVES A THRILL AND CRAWL UP THE SIDE OF THE BUILDING... UNTIL I CAN FIND AN EMPTY OFFICE... WHERE I CAN CHANGE INTO PETER PARKER!
HHMMM... MY SPIDER-SENSE ISN'T REACTING TO THIS ROOM. IT MUST BE UNOCCUPIED.
WITH MY LUCK, IT'S PROBABLY THE LADIES' LOUNGE!
HOWEVER, FATE SMILES UPON OUR AMAZING ARACHNID...
A DESERTED STOCKROOM! I COULDN'T FEEL LIKE A BIGGER CORNBALL... IF I WERE FORCED TO CHANGE IN ONE OF THOSE OLD FASHIONED TELEPHONE BOOTHS!
I'D BETTER SECURE THE DOOR. IT WOULD BE INSTANT EMBARRASSMENT IF ANYONE WALKED IN AND CAUGHT PETER PARKER IN HIS UNDEROOS!
SWAK!

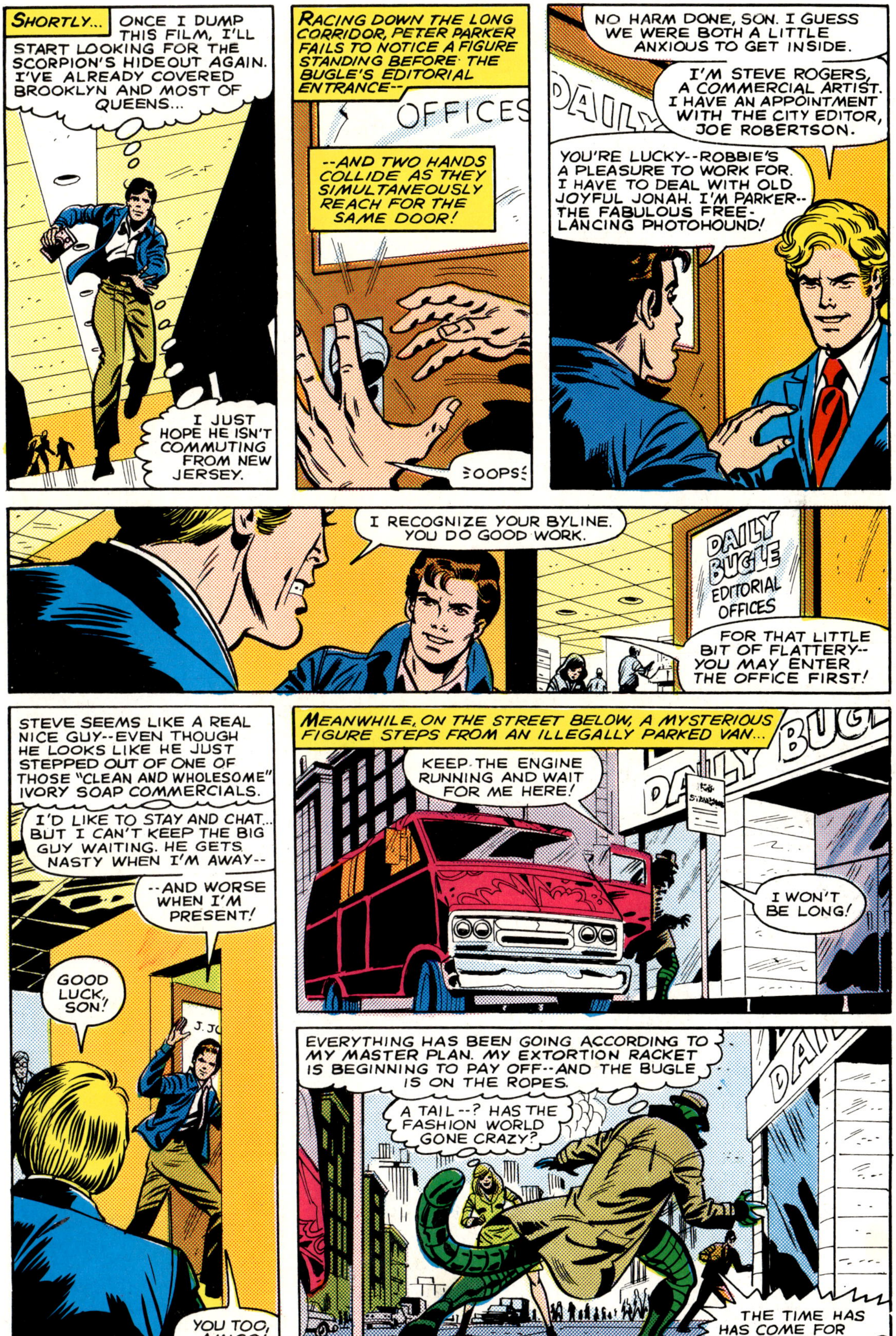
SHORTLY...
ONCE I DUMP THIS FILM, I'LL START LOOKING FOR THE SCORPION'S HIDEOUT AGAIN. I'VE ALREADY COVERED BROOKLYN AND MOST OF QUEENS...
I JUST HOPE HE ISN'T COMMUTING FROM NEW JERSEY.
RACING DOWN THE LONG CORRIDOR, PETER PARKER FAILS TO NOTICE A FIGURE STANDING BEFORE THE BUGLE'S EDITORIAL ENTRANCE--
OFFICES
--AND TWO HANDS COLLIDE AS THEY SIMULTANEOUSLY REACH FOR THE SAME DOOR!
OOPS
NO HARM DONE, SON. I GUESS WE WERE BOTH A LITTLE ANXIOUS TO GET INSIDE.
I'M STEVE ROGERS, A COMMERCIAL ARTIST. I HAVE AN APPOINTMENT WITH THE CITY EDITOR, JOE ROBERTSON.
YOU'RE LUCKY--ROBBIE'S A PLEASURE TO WORK FOR. I HAVE TO DEAL WITH OLD JOYFUL JONAH. I'M PARKER-- THE FABULOUS FREE-LANCING PHOTOHOUND!
I RECOGNIZE YOUR BYLINE. YOU DO GOOD WORK.
DAILY BUGLE EDITORIAL OFFICES
FOR THAT LITTLE BIT OF FLATTERY-- YOU MAY ENTER THE OFFICE FIRST!
STEVE SEEMS LIKE A REAL NICE GUY--EVEN THOUGH HE LOOKS LIKE HE JUST STEPPED OUT OF ONE OF THOSE "CLEAN AND WHOLESOME" IVORY SOAP COMMERCIALS.
I'D LIKE TO STAY AND CHAT... BUT I CAN'T KEEP THE BIG GUY WAITING. HE GETS NASTY WHEN I'M AWAY--
--AND WORSE WHEN I'M PRESENT!
GOOD LUCK, SON!
YOU TOO, AMIGO!
MEANWHILE, ON THE STREET BELOW, A MYSTERIOUS FIGURE STEPS FROM AN ILLEGALLY PARKED VAN...
KEEP THE ENGINE RUNNING AND WAIT FOR ME HERE!
I WON'T BE LONG!
EVERYTHING HAS BEEN GOING ACCORDING TO MY MASTER PLAN. MY EXTORTION RACKET IS BEGINNING TO PAY OFF--AND THE BUGLE IS ON THE ROPES.
A TAIL--? HAS THE FASHION WORLD GONE CRAZY?
THE TIME HAS HAS COME FOR JAMESON...TO DIE!
10

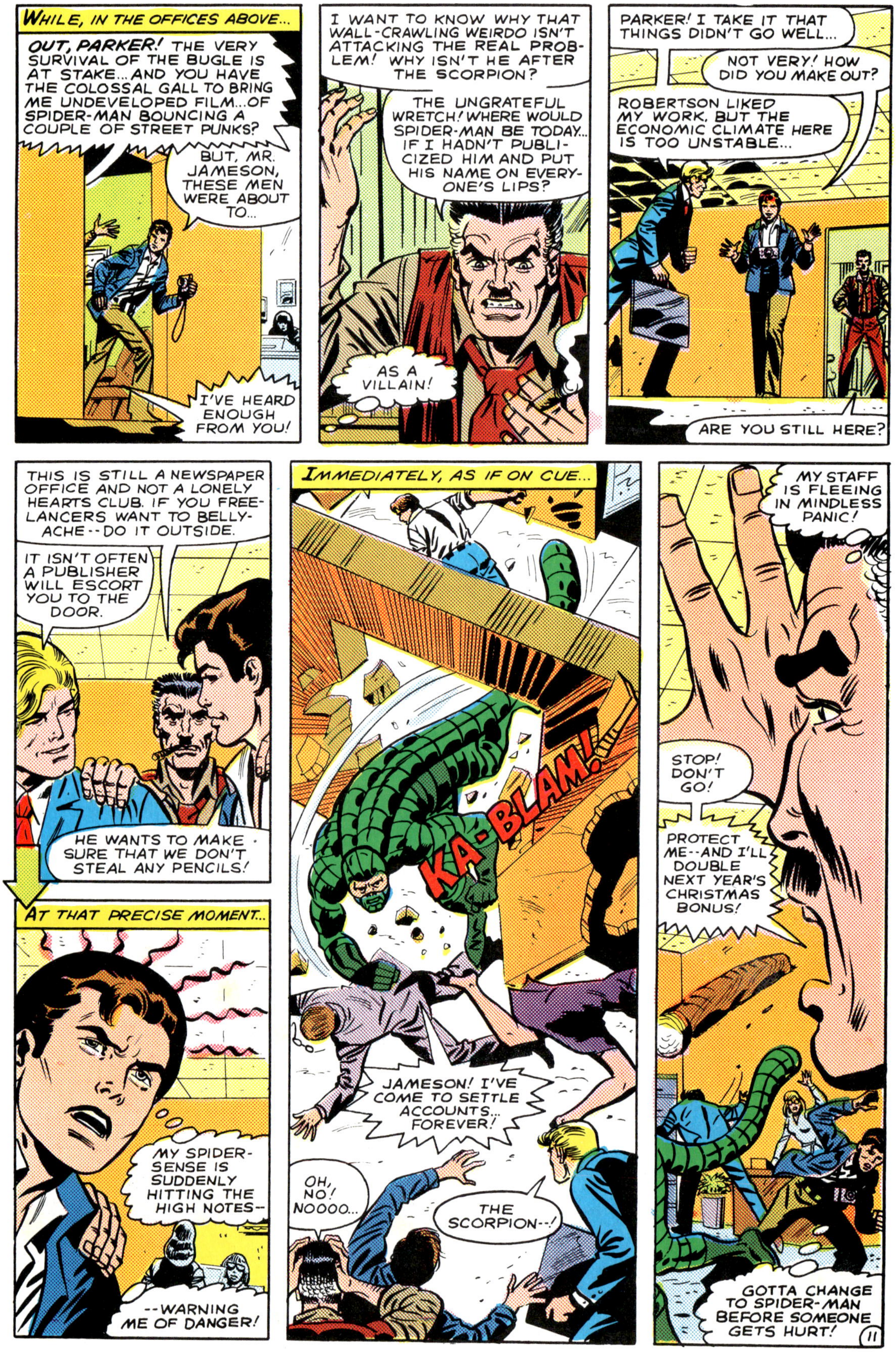
WHILE, IN THE OFFICES ABOVE...
OUT, PARKER! THE VERY SURVIVAL OF THE BUGLE IS AT STAKE...AND YOU HAVE THE COLOSSAL GALL TO BRING ME UNDEVELOPED FILM...OF SPIDER-MAN BOUNCING A COUPLE OF STREET PUNKS?
BUT, MR. JAMESON, THESE MEN WERE ABOUT TO...
I'VE HEARD ENOUGH FROM YOU!
I WANT TO KNOW WHY THAT WALL-CRAWLING WEIRDO ISN'T ATTACKING THE REAL PROBLEM! WHY ISN'T HE AFTER THE SCORPION?
THE UNGRATEFUL WRETCH! WHERE WOULD SPIDER-MAN BE TODAY... IF I HADN'T PUBLICIZED HIM AND PUT HIS NAME ON EVERYONE'S LIPS?
AS A VILLAIN!
PARKER! I TAKE IT THAT THINGS DIDN'T GO WELL...
NOT VERY! HOW DID YOU MAKE OUT?
ROBERTSON LIKED MY WORK, BUT THE ECONOMIC CLIMATE HERE IS TOO UNSTABLE...
ARE YOU STILL HERE?
THIS IS STILL A NEWSPAPER OFFICE AND NOT A LONELY HEARTS CLUB. IF YOU FREE-LANCERS WANT TO BELLY-ACHE--DO IT OUTSIDE.
IT ISN'T OFTEN A PUBLISHER WILL ESCORT YOU TO THE DOOR.
HE WANTS TO MAKE SURE THAT WE DON'T STEAL ANY PENCILS!
AT THAT PRECISE MOMENT...
MY SPIDER-SENSE IS SUDDENLY HITTING THE HIGH NOTES--
--WARNING ME OF DANGER!
IMMEDIATELY, AS IF ON CUE...
KA-BLAM!
JAMESON! I'VE COME TO SETTLE ACCOUNTS... FOREVER!
OH, NO! NOOOO...
THE SCORPION--!
MY STAFF IS FLEEING IN MINDLESS PANIC!
STOP! DON'T GO!
PROTECT ME--AND I'LL DOUBLE NEXT YEAR'S CHRISTMAS BONUS!
GOTTA CHANGE TO SPIDER-MAN BEFORE SOMEONE GETS HURT!
11

I WAS GOING TO DUCK BEHIND THOSE FILING CABINETS-- BUT I CAN SENSE THAT SOMEONE BEAT ME TO THEM!
I GUESS IT'S BACK TO THE OLD STOCK-ROOM...
AND, EVEN AS PETER PARKER JOINS THE HEADLONG STAMPEDE FOR THE EXITS--
--A STARTLING TRANSFORMATION IS TAKING PLACE... AS ARTIST STEVEN ROGERS SHEDS HIS DRAB CIVILIAN SUIT--TO REVEAL THE BRIGHTLY COLORED COSTUME OF THE CHAMPION OF FREEDOM... CAPTAIN AMERICA!
I'VE FOUGHT THE SCORPION BEFORE!* THAT'S WHY I DECIDED TO INVESTIGATE HIS LITTLE STRONG-ARM OPERATION!
*SEE CAPTAIN AMERICA #122, 151, 152.--D.
WHILE...
CLEAR OUT-- ALL OF YOU!
MY BUSINESS IS WITH JAMESON... ALONE!
ROBERTSON, PERHAPS JONAH'S ONLY TRUE FRIEND, HAS REMAINED BEHIND. FOR YEARS HE HAS SHIELDED HIS EMPLOYER FROM PETTY ANNOYANCES AND IRATE CALLERS...
NOW, HE DESPERATELY ATTEMPTS TO SHIELD HIM FROM DEATH--
--AND FAILS, MOST DECIDEDLY!
ROBBIE!
KWOK!
I'LL NEVER FORGIVE MYSELF IF HE'S COME TO HARM ON MY ACCOUNT!
GARGAN, LISTEN! I'LL GIVE ANYTHING... PAY ANY PRICE, IF ONLY YOU'LL LEAVE ME ALONE!
I TOOK YOUR BLOODY MONEY ONCE--AND LOOK WHAT IT DID TO ME! I OUGHTTA...
OH, NO--!
CAPTAIN AMERICA! BUT I WAS EXPECTING THE WEB-SPINNER...
I'M A HERO, NOT A POLITICIAN! I DON'T ARGUE JURISDICTION WHILE LIVES ARE IN DANGER!
GET HIM, CAP!
WHERE DO THESE LONG-JOHNED JERKS COME FROM? IF I DIDN'T KNOW BETTER, I'D SWEAR THIS ONE WAS HIDING IN MY COAT CLOSET!
12

BACK OFF, YOU SHIELD-SLINGING STOOGE! NO MERE MAN CAN SURVIVE AGAINST A MONSTER LIKE... UGGG
THIS "MERE MAN" HAS FOUGHT MANY SO-CALLED "MONSTERS" IN HIS DAY... AND EMERGED VICTORIOUS!
TWAP!
MOST OF THE OTHERS LACKED YOUR GAUDY COSTUME AND SUPER-STRENGTH--
--BUT THEY SHARED YOUR BRUTAL DISREGARD FOR HUMAN LIFE AND LIBERTY!
HE'S FAR STRONGER AND FASTER THAN ME -- BUT I CAN KEEP HIM ON THE DEFENSIVE BY HAMMERING AWAY AT HIM WITH MY SHIELD!
HOWEVER, MOVING ALMOST FASTER THAN THE EYE CAN FOLLOW, THE SCORPION WHIRLS ABOUT, AND SENDS HIS BONE-CRUSHING TAIL TO SLASH AT THE VALIANT AVENGER...
SHUT UP! IF I WANTED A SERMON, I'D MUG A MINISTER!
HIS TAIL IS AN AWESOME WEAPON--BUT I GOT BENEATH IT... IN TIME!
WOW! LOOK WHO SHOWED UP WHILE I WAS GONE!
UH-OH! OLD WINGHEAD LOOKS LIKE HE'S IN TROUBLE!
INDEED!
THERE! I TAGGED YA BEFORE YOU RE-GAINED YOUR BALANCE!
UNNN I MANAGED TO LESSEN THE BLOW BY ROLLING WITH IT... BUT I'LL STILL NEED A FEW SECONDS TO RECOVER!
13

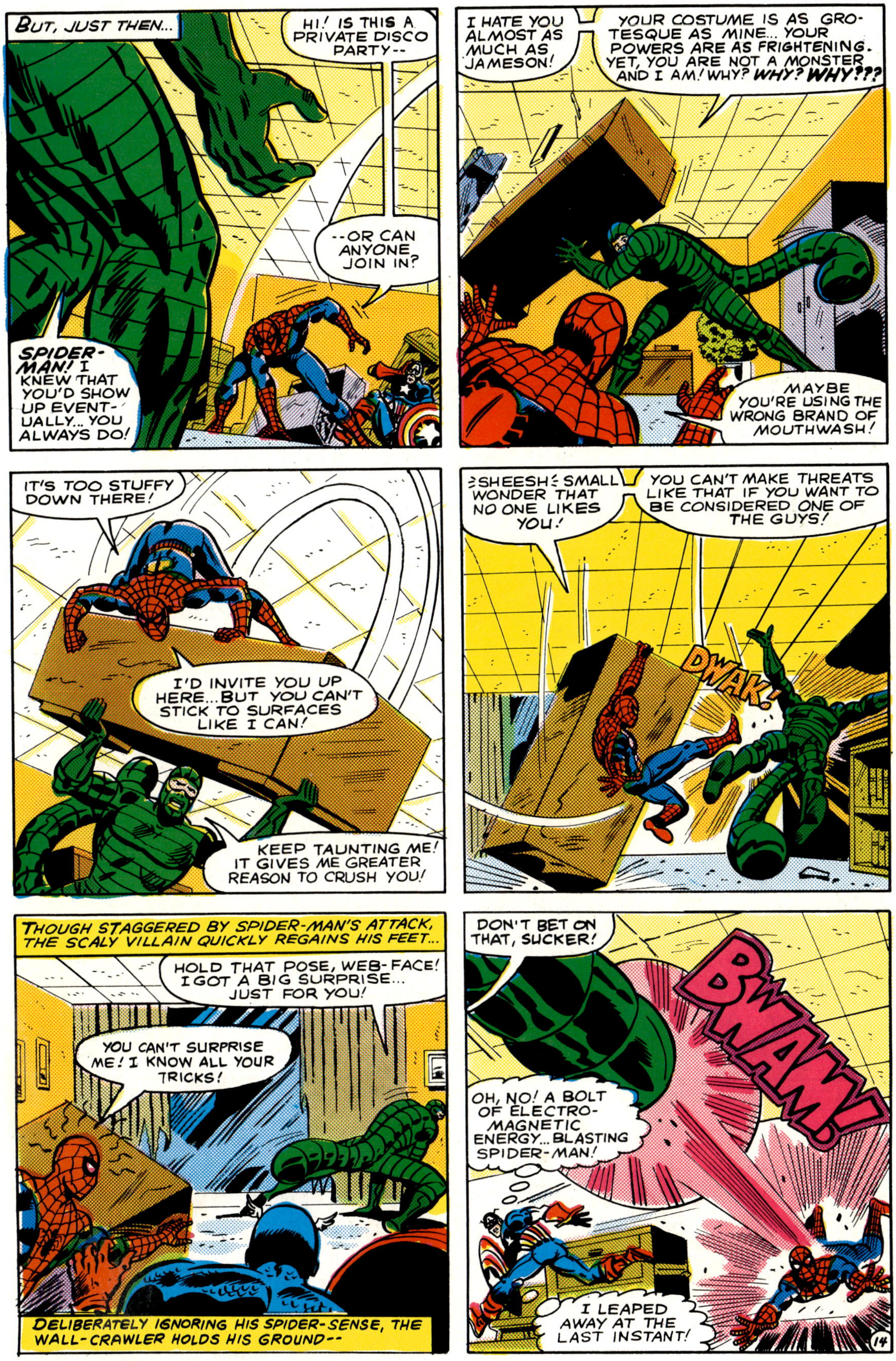

BUT, JUST THEN...
HI! IS THIS A PRIVATE DISCO PARTY--
--OR CAN ANYONE JOIN IN?
SPIDER-MAN! I KNEW THAT YOU'D SHOW UP EVENT-UALLY... YOU ALWAYS DO!
I HATE YOU ALMOST AS MUCH AS JAMESON!
YOUR COSTUME IS AS GRO-TESQUE AS MINE... YOUR POWERS ARE AS FRIGHTENING. YET, YOU ARE NOT A MONSTER AND I AM! WHY? WHY? WHY???
MAYBE YOU'RE USING THE WRONG BRAND OF MOUTHWASH!
IT'S TOO STUFFY DOWN THERE!
I'D INVITE YOU UP HERE... BUT YOU CAN'T STICK TO SURFACES LIKE I CAN!
KEEP TAUNTING ME! IT GIVES ME GREATER REASON TO CRUSH YOU!
≥SHEESH≤ SMALL WONDER THAT NO ONE LIKES YOU!
YOU CAN'T MAKE THREATS LIKE THAT IF YOU WANT TO BE CONSIDERED ONE OF THE GUYS!
DWAK!
THOUGH STAGGERED BY SPIDER-MAN'S ATTACK, THE SCALY VILLAIN QUICKLY REGAINS HIS FEET...
HOLD THAT POSE, WEB-FACE! I GOT A BIG SURPRISE... JUST FOR YOU!
YOU CAN'T SURPRISE ME! I KNOW ALL YOUR TRICKS!
DELIBERATELY IGNORING HIS SPIDER-SENSE, THE WALL-CRAWLER HOLDS HIS GROUND--
DON'T BET ON THAT, SUCKER!
BWAM!
OH, NO! A BOLT OF ELECTRO-MAGNETIC ENERGY... BLASTING SPIDER-MAN!
I LEAPED AWAY AT THE LAST INSTANT!
14

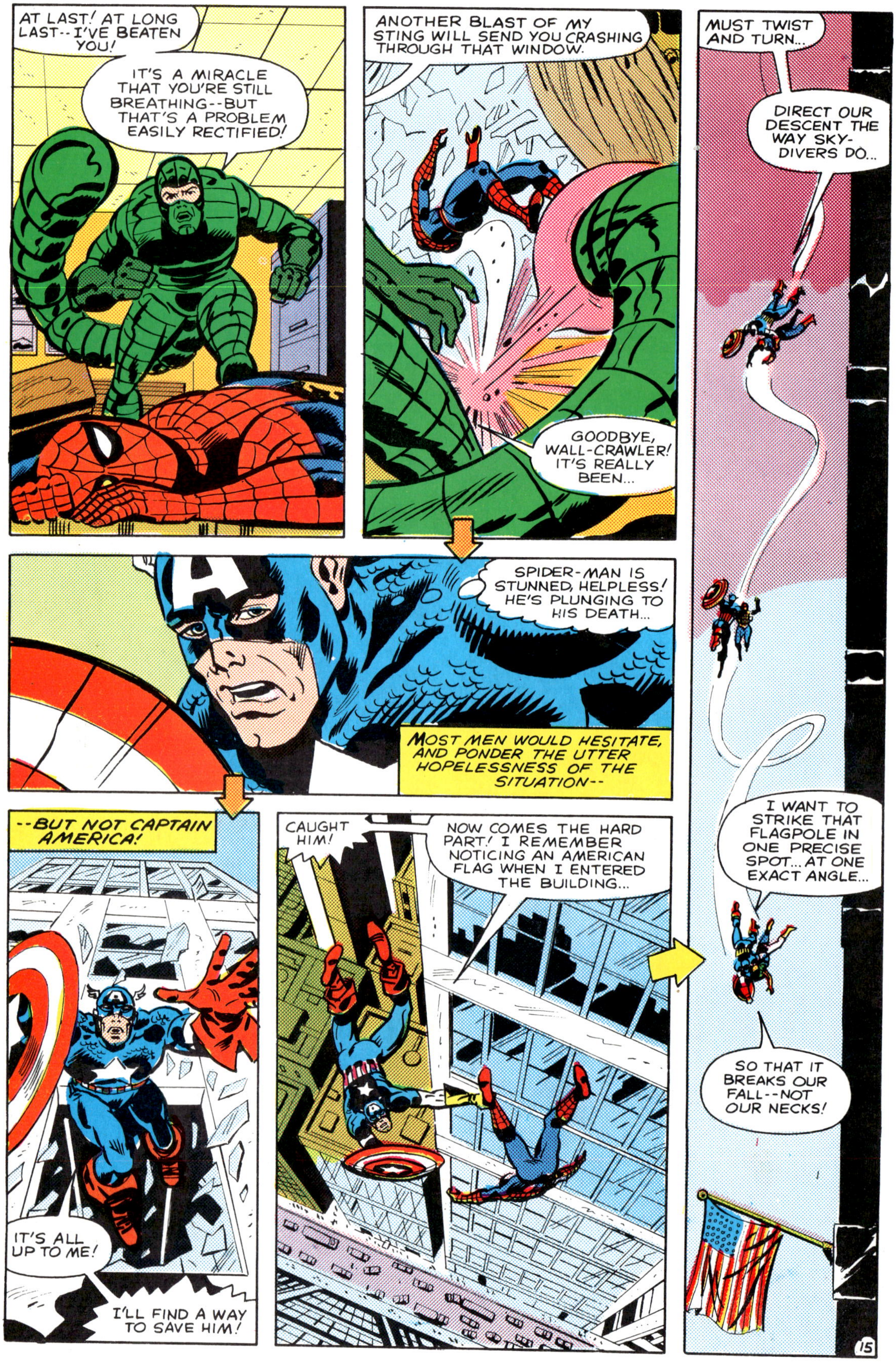

AT LAST! AT LONG LAST--I'VE BEATEN YOU!
IT'S A MIRACLE THAT YOU'RE STILL BREATHING--BUT THAT'S A PROBLEM EASILY RECTIFIED!
ANOTHER BLAST OF MY STING WILL SEND YOU CRASHING THROUGH THAT WINDOW.
GOODBYE, WALL-CRAWLER! IT'S REALLY BEEN...
MUST TWIST AND TURN...
DIRECT OUR DESCENT THE WAY SKY-DIVERS DO...
SPIDER-MAN IS STUNNED, HELPLESS! HE'S PLUNGING TO HIS DEATH...
MOST MEN WOULD HESITATE, AND PONDER THE UTTER HOPELESSNESS OF THE SITUATION--
--BUT NOT CAPTAIN AMERICA!
IT'S ALL UP TO ME!
I'LL FIND A WAY TO SAVE HIM!
CAUGHT HIM!
NOW COMES THE HARD PART! I REMEMBER NOTICING AN AMERICAN FLAG WHEN I ENTERED THE BUILDING...
I WANT TO STRIKE THAT FLAGPOLE IN ONE PRECISE SPOT...AT ONE EXACT ANGLE...
SO THAT IT BREAKS OUR FALL--NOT OUR NECKS!

THIS IS IT! MY SHIELD SHOULD CUSHION A FAIR AMOUNT OF THE IMPACT...
CWAP!
YAHOO! I KNEW I COULD DEPEND ON THE OLD STARS AND STRIPES... BUT WE'RE NOT OUT OF DANGER YET.
TWANG!
WE COULD STILL BE SPLATTERED ACROSS THE SIDEWALK IF I CAN'T AIM US FOR THAT NEARBY STORE AWNING--
--AND THE CLOTHING DISPLAY BENEATH IT!
BWUMP!
THEY'RE BOTH DEAD! THEY'VE GOT TO BE!
NO ONE COULD HAVE SURVIVED A FALL LIKE THAT!
I STAYED BEHIND SO THAT I COULD CLAIM TO BE IN ON THE SCORPION'S CAPTURE--
--BUT THOSE BLASTED HEROES FAILED ME!
HOLD IT, JAMESON! I HAVEN'T FORGOTTEN YOU!
DO YOU HAVE ANY IDEA OF WHAT I'VE SUFFERED BECAUSE OF YOU? FOR YEARS I THOUGHT MY COSTUME COULDN'T COME OFF. WHEN IT FINALLY DID, I DISCOVERED THAT I COULDN'T LIVE WITHOUT IT!
YOU CAN'T BLAME THAT ON ME!
CAN'T I?
YOU'RE COMING WITH ME. I'M GOING TO COLLECT FOR ALL OF MY TORMENT...ALL OF MY MANY YEARS OF SENSELESS AGONY...
BUT YOU'LL NEED MORE THAN MONEY TO PAY THIS BILL!
OOOH! CAN'T STOP HIM FROM TAKING JONAH...
16

MEANWHILE...
NEVER SAW ANYTHING LIKE IT! THEY JUST FELL OUTTA THE SKY!
IT'S A MIRACLE... THAT THEY'RE STILL ALIVE!
BUT WHAT'S A RESPECTED AVENGER DOING WITH A LOSER LIKE SPIDER-MAN?
MY ADORING PUBLIC!
CAP! I DON'T KNOW HOW TO...
FORGET IT, SON! IT'S ALL PART OF THE SERVICE!
HEY!!! YOU LUNATICS COULDA KILLED SOMEBODY WITH THAT CRAZY STUNT! I'M GONNA SUE FOR THE CLOTHES YOU RUINED.
SUBMIT A BILL TO AVENGERS MANSION, AND I'LL SEE THAT YOU'RE COMPENSATED, I'M SORRY FOR ANY...
ER... MORE TROUBLE, AMIGO!
THAT'S JOE ROBERTSON HANGING OUT OF THAT UPPER FLOOR WINDOW. I CAN'T MAKE OUT THE WORDS... BUT FROM HIS TONE, I'D GUESS THAT THE SCORPION MADE OFF WITH JAMESON!
SPIDER-MAN MUST HAVE INCREDIBLE RECUPERATIVE POWERS. HE'S ALREADY SHAKEN OFF THE EFFECTS OF THE ELECTRO-SHOCK AND THE FALL.
I'LL NEED A FEW MINUTES TO HAVE THIS ARM TAPED... I MIGHT HAVE SPRAINED IT WHEN WE LANDED.
EVENTUALLY...
WOW! PEOPLE WERE FALLING OVER THEMSELVES IN AN EFFORT TO HELP CAP THEY EVEN DESCRIBED THE SCORPION'S ESCAPE VEHICLE AND THE DIRECTION IT TOOK...
ᵹ SIGH ᵹ WHY COULDN'T I HAVE BEEN BITTEN BY A RADIOACTIVE APPLE PIE?

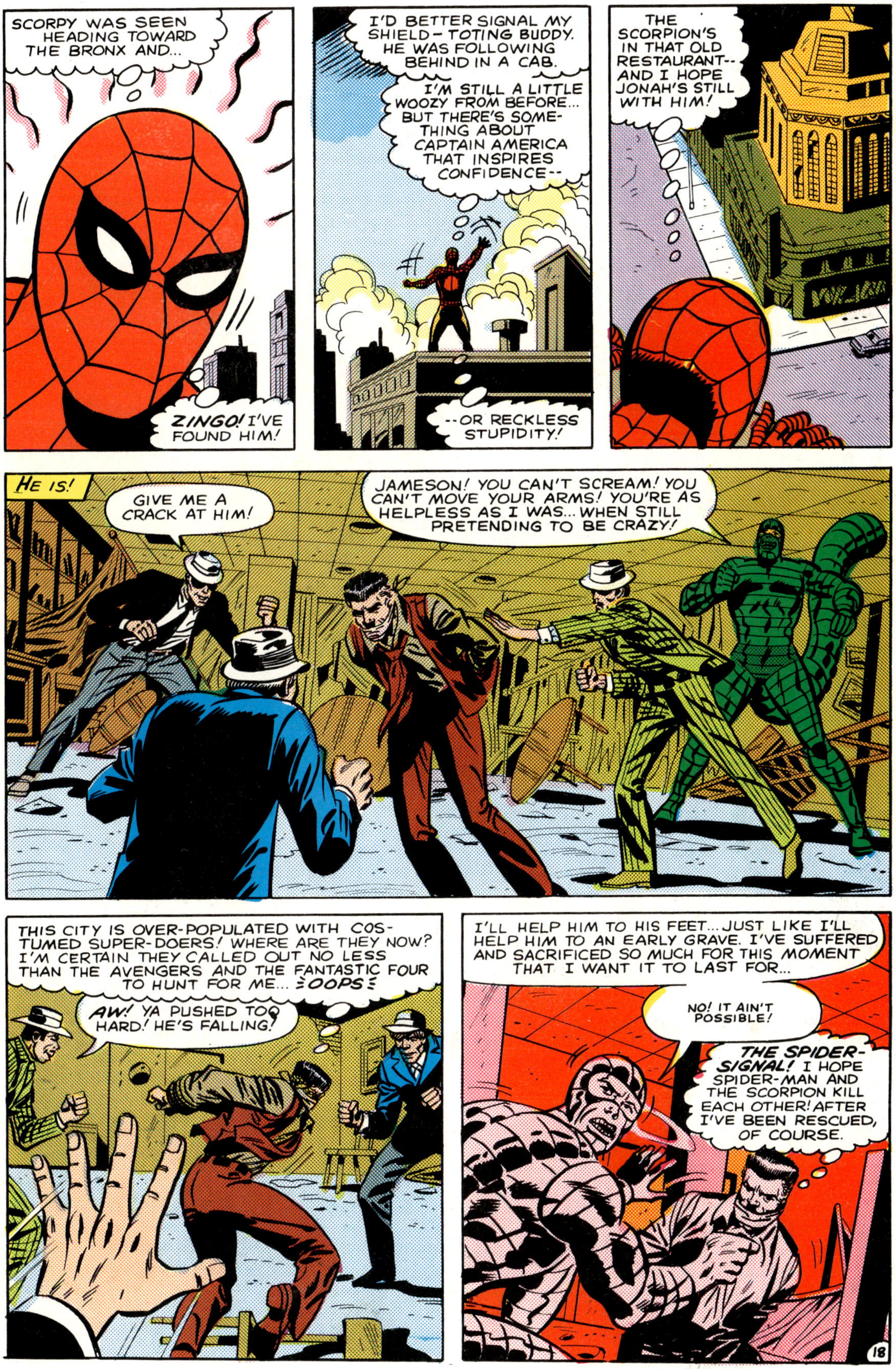
SCORPY WAS SEEN HEADING TOWARD THE BRONX AND...
ZINGO! I'VE FOUND HIM!
I'D BETTER SIGNAL MY SHIELD-TOTING BUDDY. HE WAS FOLLOWING BEHIND IN A CAB.
I'M STILL A LITTLE WOOZY FROM BEFORE... BUT THERE'S SOMETHING ABOUT CAPTAIN AMERICA THAT INSPIRES CONFIDENCE--
--OR RECKLESS STUPIDITY!
THE SCORPION'S IN THAT OLD RESTAURANT-- AND I HOPE JONAH'S STILL WITH HIM!
HE IS!
GIVE ME A CRACK AT HIM!
JAMESON! YOU CAN'T SCREAM! YOU CAN'T MOVE YOUR ARMS! YOU'RE AS HELPLESS AS I WAS... WHEN STILL PRETENDING TO BE CRAZY!
THIS CITY IS OVER-POPULATED WITH COSTUMED SUPER-DOERS! WHERE ARE THEY NOW? I'M CERTAIN THEY CALLED OUT NO LESS THAN THE AVENGERS AND THE FANTASTIC FOUR TO HUNT FOR ME... OOPS
AW! YA PUSHED TOO HARD! HE'S FALLING!
I'LL HELP HIM TO HIS FEET... JUST LIKE I'LL HELP HIM TO AN EARLY GRAVE. I'VE SUFFERED AND SACRIFICED SO MUCH FOR THIS MOMENT THAT I WANT IT TO LAST FOR...
NO! IT AIN'T POSSIBLE!
THE SPIDER-SIGNAL! I HOPE SPIDER-MAN AND THE SCORPION KILL EACH OTHER! AFTER I'VE BEEN RESCUED, OF COURSE.
18

YESSIREE! HE LIVES! HE BREATHES! HE FLOATS THROUGH THE AIR WITH THE GREATEST OF EASE!
IT'S SPIDER-MAN! NAIL 'IM-- BEFORE HE SLAUGHTERS US!
JUST THEN, APPROPRIATING A SERVING CART FROM THE RESTAURANT'S BACK ROOM, CAPTAIN AMERICA STREAKS INTO THE FRAY LIKE A METEOR...
A GUNMAN IS AIMING AT THE WEB-HEAD!
THROWN WITH UNNERVING ACCURACY, CAPTAIN AMERICA'S SHIELD EASILY DISPOSES OF THE UNWARY ASSASSIN...
MUCH OBLIGED, EL CAPITAN!
MY SPIDER-SENSE WARNED ME OF THE DANGER-- BUT I APPRECIATE THE ASSIST!
SUDDENLY, UNEXPECTEDLY...
USE YOUR WEAPONS, MEN! DISPOSE OF THESE COSTUMED CLOWNS... WHILE I ATTEND TO JAMESON!
IS HE KIDDING??? WE'RE SUPPOSED TO TAKE ON THE HEAVIES--WHILE HE BEATS A RETREAT???
LIFE CAN BE SO UNFAIR!
EXCUSE ME... WHILE I PUT YOUR HEAD TO MORE USE THAN YOU EVER DID...
I'VE GOT TO STOP THAT GREEN-SKINNED GUMDROP BEFORE HE CREATES A RECIPE FOR PUBLISHER PANCAKES!

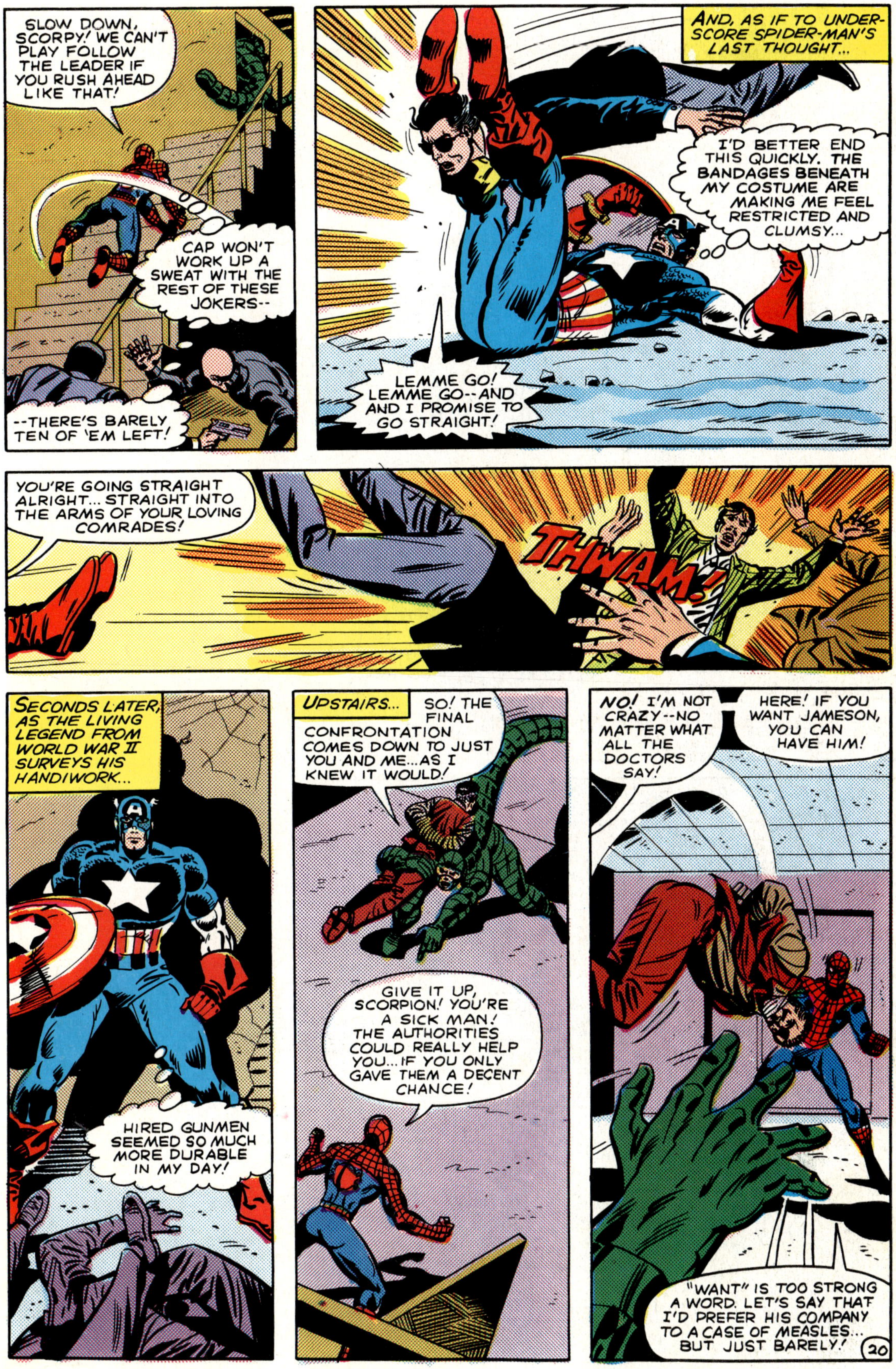
SLOW DOWN, SCORPY! WE CAN'T PLAY FOLLOW THE LEADER IF YOU RUSH AHEAD LIKE THAT!
CAP WON'T WORK UP A SWEAT WITH THE REST OF THESE JOKERS--
--THERE'S BARELY TEN OF 'EM LEFT!
AND, AS IF TO UNDERSCORE SPIDER-MAN'S LAST THOUGHT...
I'D BETTER END THIS QUICKLY. THE BANDAGES BENEATH MY COSTUME ARE MAKING ME FEEL RESTRICTED AND CLUMSY...
LEMME GO! LEMME GO--AND AND I PROMISE TO GO STRAIGHT!
YOU'RE GOING STRAIGHT ALRIGHT... STRAIGHT INTO THE ARMS OF YOUR LOVING COMRADES!
THWAM!
SECONDS LATER, AS THE LIVING LEGEND FROM WORLD WAR II SURVEYS HIS HANDIWORK...
HIRED GUNMEN SEEMED SO MUCH MORE DURABLE IN MY DAY!
UPSTAIRS...
SO! THE FINAL CONFRONTATION COMES DOWN TO JUST YOU AND ME... AS I KNEW IT WOULD!
GIVE IT UP, SCORPION! YOU'RE A SICK MAN! THE AUTHORITIES COULD REALLY HELP YOU... IF YOU ONLY GAVE THEM A DECENT CHANCE!
NO! I'M NOT CRAZY--NO MATTER WHAT ALL THE DOCTORS SAY!
HERE! IF YOU WANT JAMESON, YOU CAN HAVE HIM!
"WANT" IS TOO STRONG A WORD. LET'S SAY THAT I'D PREFER HIS COMPANY TO A CASE OF MEASLES... BUT JUST BARELY!
20

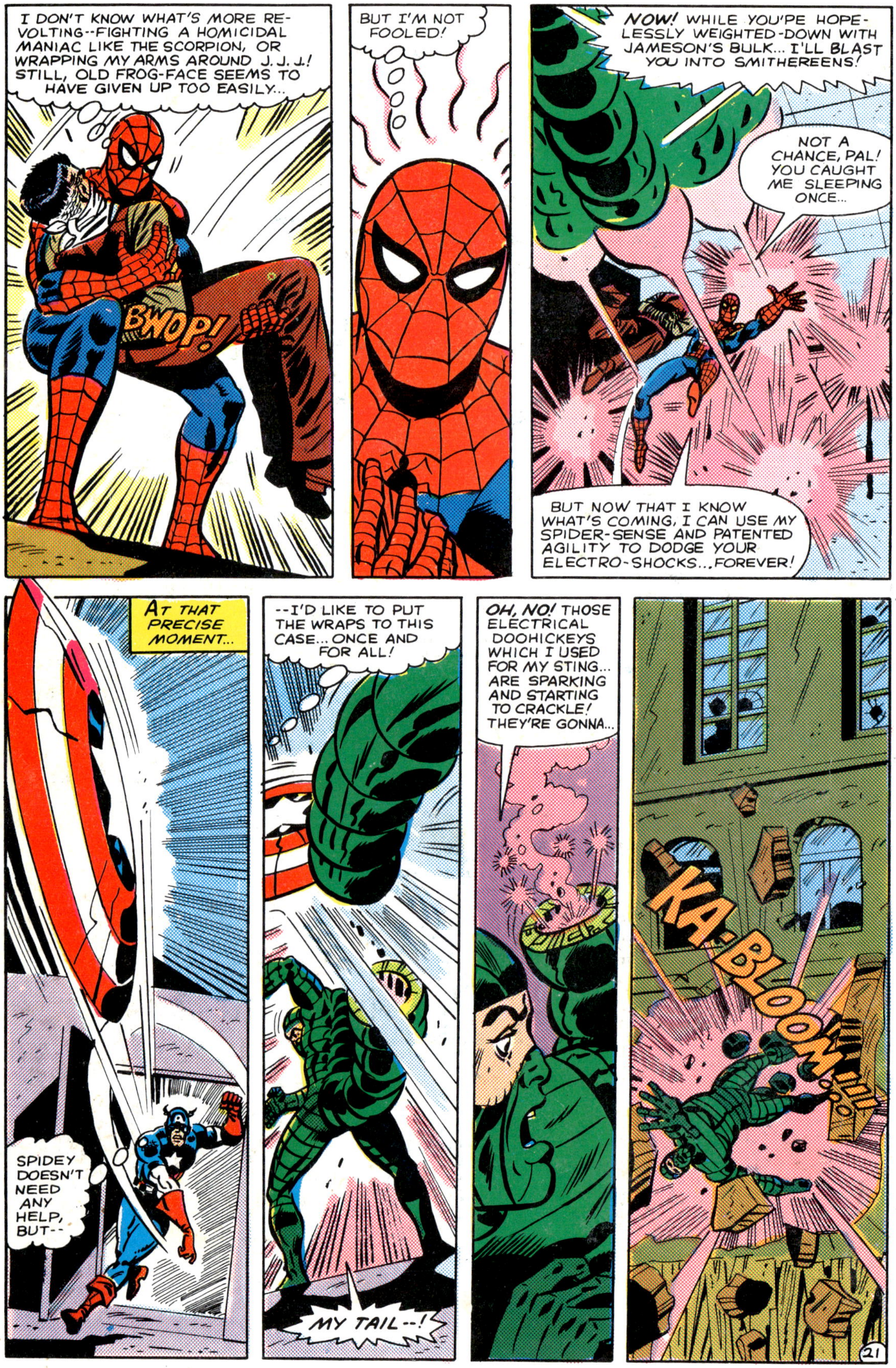
I DON'T KNOW WHAT'S MORE REVOLTING--FIGHTING A HOMICIDAL MANIAC LIKE THE SCORPION, OR WRAPPING MY ARMS AROUND J. J. J.! STILL, OLD FROG-FACE SEEMS TO HAVE GIVEN UP TOO EASILY...
BWOP!
BUT I'M NOT FOOLED!
NOW! WHILE YOU'RE HOPELESSLY WEIGHTED-DOWN WITH JAMESON'S BULK... I'LL BLAST YOU INTO SMITHEREENS!
NOT A CHANCE, PAL! YOU CAUGHT ME SLEEPING ONCE...
BUT NOW THAT I KNOW WHAT'S COMING, I CAN USE MY SPIDER-SENSE AND PATENTED AGILITY TO DODGE YOUR ELECTRO-SHOCKS... FOREVER!
AT THAT PRECISE MOMENT...
SPIDEY DOESN'T NEED ANY HELP, BUT--
--I'D LIKE TO PUT THE WRAPS TO THIS CASE... ONCE AND FOR ALL!
MY TAIL--!
OH, NO! THOSE ELECTRICAL DOOHICKEYS WHICH I USED FOR MY STING... ARE SPARKING AND STARTING TO CRACKLE! THEY'RE GONNA...
KA-BLOOM!!!!!